75 Hikes in™

CALIFORNIA'S
Lassen Park &
Mount Shasta Regions

75 Hikes in™

CALIFORNIA'S
Lassen Park &
Mount Shasta Regions

John R. Soares

THE
MOUNTAINEERS

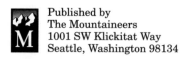
Published by
The Mountaineers
1001 SW Klickitat Way
Seattle, Washington 98134

09876
54321

Published simultaneously in Canada by Douglas & McIntyre, Ltd., 1615 Venables Street, Vancouver, B.C. V5L 2H1

Published simultaneously in Great Britain by Cordee, 3a DeMontfort Street, Leicester, England, LE1 7HD

Manufactured in the United States of America

Edited by Sarah Lane
Maps by Nick Gregoric
All photographs by the author unless otherwise noted
Cover design by The Mountaineers Books
Book design and typography by The Mountaineers Books
Book layout by Michelle Taverniti

Cover photograph: *Mount Shasta from the south* © Andy Selters
Frontispiece: *Mill Creek Falls*

Library of Congress Cataloging-in-Publication Data

Soares, John R.
    75 hikes in California's Lassen Park & Mount Shasta regions / John R. Soares.
        p.   cm.
    Includes bibliographical references (p.).
    ISBN 0-89886-466-6
    1. Hiking—California—Lassen Volcanic Park—Guidebooks. 2. Hiking—California—Shasta, Mount (Mountain)—Guidebooks. 3. Lassen Volcanic National Park (Calif.)—Guidebooks. 4. Shasta, Mount (Calif. : Mountain)—Guidebooks I. Title.
GV199.42.C22L3783   1996
796.5'2'0979424—dc20   95–52902
                                                                      CIP

CONTENTS

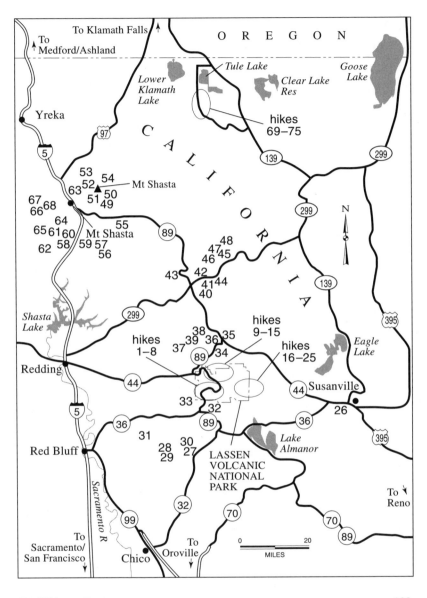

ACKNOWLEDGMENTS

For Noelle: my wife, my best friend, my soul mate

The most appreciation goes to my wife Noelle, who hiked many of the trails with me and who understands and shares my love of nature. My brother Marc J. Soares often accompanied me and provided research and photos for three hikes—many thanks. Other special people who walked with me include my sister Camille Soares, my brother Eric J. Soares, and my good friend Rick Ramos. Jack Hathaway, Abe Hathaway, Abbie Hathaway, and Kris Hathaway provided valuable advice about the trails at Crystal and Baum lakes. I also thank the following for their love and support: my mother Mozelle Berta, my stepfather Les Berta, Bill Phelps, Lucy Phelps, and Craig Heath. I give deep gratitude to the rangers and naturalists who answered my many questions and agreed to review the manuscript, especially Scott Isaacson, Betty Knight, Steve Zachary, and Nancy Bailey at Lassen Volcanic National Park; Lisa Sedlacek of the Almanor Ranger District; Stan Bales of the Bureau of Land Management's Eagle Lake Resource Area, Kathy Turner and Jim Barnhart of the Hat Creek Ranger District; Adria Schulz of PG&E; Steve Moore of McArthur-Burney Falls Memorial State Park; Don Lee of the Mount Shasta Ranger District; Barbara Paolinetti of the McCloud Ranger District; Fred Welcome of Castle Crags State Park; and Gary Hathaway of Lava Beds National Monument. Of course, any errors in the book are entirely my responsibility.

Buckeye trees sport long spikes of white flowers in spring.

INTRODUCTION

Over millions of years, powerful forces emanating from deep in the earth have shoved the floor of the Pacific Ocean under much of the west coast of the United States, heating and liquefying vast quantities of rock that reached the earth's surface to form the Cascades. *75 Hikes in California's Lassen Park and Mount Shasta Regions* details all your hiking options in northern California's portion of this vast and beautiful volcanic landscape; it guides you to the summits of Mount Shasta and Lassen Peak, along the shores of dozens of beautiful backwoods lakes, through verdant meadows vibrant with wildflowers, and to numerous waterfalls, large and small. This book is your ticket to all that is wild and wonderful in Lassen Volcanic National Park, Caribou Wilderness, Ishi Wilderness, Lassen National Forest, Thousand Lakes Wilderness, McArthur-Burney Falls Memorial State Park, Ahjumawi Lava Springs State Park, Mount Shasta Wilderness, Shasta-Trinity National Forest, Castle Crags State Park, Castle Crags Wilderness, and Lava Beds National Monument. Enjoy.

How to Use This Book

The main portion of each hike description covers directions to the trailhead, distances between trail forks and major landmarks, location of campsites, and natural and human history of the area. The beginning of each hike description has a list of important information that gives you a basic feel for what you're undertaking. Here is what this information means:

Length. This is the hike's round trip distance. Most hikes reach beautiful destinations within a mile or two, so if time or energy are in short supply, read through to find the nearby waterfall, meadow, or open view that will satisfy your yearning.

Hiking time. This is calculated to give the average hiker plenty of time to rest, eat, and delight in nature.

High point. This is the elevation in feet of the highest place the trail reaches.

Total elevation gain. Taking into account all the ups and downs of the trail, this shows you how many actual feet you'll climb.

Difficulty. The designations *easy, moderate,* and *strenuous* were determined by combining length, total elevation gain, agility needed, and amount of effort needed. Most folks will have no problems on an easy hike; carefully judge your ability and preparedness and those of your companions before beginning moderate and strenuous hikes. Note that many hikes with the latter two designations require little effort for the first couple of miles to a beautiful turnaround point.

Season. This gives the months in an "average" year that you can access the trailhead and do the hike without encountering significant amounts of snow. A heavy winter or an early autumn storm will shrink this window; conversely, a mild winter prolongs it. Trails in Castle Crags State Park and McArthur-Burney Falls Memorial State Park, and along the McCloud River and Hat Creek, often have snow-free periods during winter months. Always call the government agency with jurisdiction (described in Appendix 1) if you're at all unsure about the hikability of a trail. Hike on weekdays and in the off-season if you desire solitude.

Water. This indicates streams and lakes along the trail that can serve as sources of drinking water, although these will sometimes dry up in late summer or autumn, especially in drought years. You must properly purify all water obtained in the outdoors (see **Water** in the *Safety* section). It's usually best to pack in all the water you need for day hikes to save yourself the hassle of purifying, but you should always bring iodine tablets for emergencies.

Maps. The map accompanying each hike description is for reference purposes only, although it will be adequate in most cases. The listed United States Geological Survey (USGS) and United States Forest Service (USFS) topographical maps provide many more details of the terrain. Buy them at outdoor supply stores, engineering supply stores, or, in the case of USFS maps, at USFS ranger stations. Some USGS maps are old and will not accurately represent the current trail system; the USFS maps are generally accurate. You also can purchase USFS maps of Lassen National Forest and Shasta-Trinity National Forest that show most roads and many trails and are very helpful in navigating back roads. Castle Crags State Park and McArthur-Burney Falls Memorial State Park sell brochures that include a detailed map of all trails.

Permit. This lets you know whether a wilderness permit is needed for the hike. Obtain the permit from the agency listed under **Information** unless otherwise noted.

You also must have a permit to have a fire or operate a stove on national forest lands. Obtain this permit from national forest offices (such as ranger district offices), Bureau of Land Management offices, and California Division of Forestry offices. Often, seasonal restrictions are placed on fires and stoves; call the relevant agency listed under **Information** for current regulations.

Nearest campground. This lists the closest campground. See Appendix 2 for details on campgrounds. For a more thorough discussion of your camping options, consult Tom Stienstra's *California Camping* (San Francisco: Foghorn Press, updated yearly).

Information. This indicates the government agency with jurisdiction over the trail. Call or drop by for information about trail conditions and access and to obtain maps, natural history handouts, and wilderness permits. Appendix 1 contains agency addresses and phone numbers.

Driving directions. Located in the second paragraph of text for each hike, these lead you to the trailhead from the nearest town or highway. Two-wheel-drive vehicles can safely reach all the trailheads, assuming that no recent storm has made dirt roads too slick or covered them with snow. Odometer meters can vary slightly, so start looking for described road junctions and similar landmarks before reaching the mileage mentioned in the text. Also, look out for those large logging trucks when traveling national forest roads.

Trailhead theft. Lower the probability that this rare event will happen to you by locking all doors, tightly closing all windows, and taking all valuables with you, including your keys and wallet or purse.

Fees. Lassen Volcanic National Park, McArthur-Burney Falls Memorial State Park, Castle Crags State Park, and Lava Beds National Monument charge an entrance fee.

What to Take

The Ten Essentials. The prudent hiker always brings extra clothing, extra food, a first-aid kit, fire starter (for wet wood), matches (in a waterproof container), a knife (for making kindling and for first aid), sunglasses, good maps, a compass, and a flashlight (with extra bulbs and batteries). Also bring water, a filter or chemicals for purifying water, a watch, toilet paper, and an emergency signaling device (mirror, whistle, or brightly colored cloth or plastic). Appendix 3 provides complete lists of supplies for both the day hiker and the backpacker.

Clothing. Always be prepared for cold temperatures and nasty weather by bringing—at minimum—pants, a sweatshirt, a watchman's cap, and a poncho. Also bring a wide-brimmed hat, sunglasses, and sunblock rated SPF 15 or higher for protection from the sun. Most folks find that a lightweight pair of hiking boots provides good traction and ankle protection, although for many hikes on dirt trails a comfortable pair of running shoes serves almost as well.

Safety

The world is a beautiful place, but it contains potential dangers. Wilderness is no exception. This section provides the basics of wilderness safety, but you should supplement your knowledge by taking courses and reading books.

Traveling alone. This certainly has its rewards, but it requires that you not take chances on stream crossings and cross-country travel, and that you be constantly alert. Always tell someone of your itinerary and expected time of return, then confirm your safe arrival when the hike's over.

Know your limitations. Don't overestimate your preparedness, physical conditioning, and agility or that of your hiking companions. Play it safe.

Weather. Get the forecast before you hike, preferably from a cable weather channel or by calling the National Weather Service. A poncho or a space blanket in your pack provides good insurance against an unexpected rainstorm and can make a day hiker's unplanned night in the wilderness safer and more pleasant. If you're backpacking, bring a good tent, a sleeping pad, and a sleeping bag rated for temperatures below your worst-case estimates. Thunderstorms appear year-round but occur most frequently in spring and summer. If those tall thunderheads show up, wait out the storm (or potential storm) among the shorter trees in the nearest forest; avoid exposed ridges and mountaintops.

Hypothermia. A big drop in body temperature characterizes this physical condition, which is usually caused by a combination of wetness, cold, wind, and fatigue. To avoid this life threatener, stay dry, bring plenty of warm clothes and a windbreaker, and stay well within your physical limits and those of your companions. Symptoms of hypothermia include shivering, loss of coordination, and inarticulate speech. If you or a companion exhibit these symptoms, seek shelter away from wind and wetness, put on dry clothes, build a fire, get in a sleeping bag (with a companion for warmth, if necessary), and eat foods high in carbohydrates (grains, breads, candy).

Water. Always assume that water sources in the wild (excluding campground faucets, unless posted otherwise) are contaminated with *Giardia*, a microorganism that causes severe intestinal distress. Avoid infection by using one of the following methods: boiling all water for at least 1 minute, treating all water with iodine or other chemicals, or filtering all water with high-quality filtration devices. Outdoor stores sell the chemicals and filtration devices. At the beginning of each hike description, you'll find information about the availability of water near the trail. Day hikers may find it most convenient to bring plenty of water from home.

Ticks. These critters typically live in brushy and grassy areas, where they hope to catch a ride with an animal (such as you) so they can bore in and drink some fresh blood. The problem: Some carry Lyme disease, which can make you very ill. You can drastically lower the odds of a tick attaching to you by wearing a long-sleeve shirt along with pants that you've tucked inside your socks. If a tick does attach, you can try to dislodge it with a tick removal kit, or you can head for the nearest doctor. If you feel any symptoms after a tick bite, definitely visit a doctor.

Rattlesnakes. Identified primarily by a jointed tail rattle, these reptiles possess a potentially fatal bite, though they'll bite only if cornered or touched. Active in the warmer months in and around summer, they live below 6,000 feet under brush and in dry rocky areas. Prevent bites by always looking where you're going and by being particularly careful where you place your hands and feet when hiking cross-country. If a rattlesnake bites you, stay calm and relaxed and get to a hospital as soon as possible.

Black bears. Most black bears will zoom away at warp speed when they spot you. The main danger occurs when a hiker passes between a mother and her cubs. If you're confronted by a bear, speak in a calm voice about your peaceful intentions as you slowly back away; do not turn and run. If an attack appears imminent, fall into the fetal position and play dead. Often the bear will lose interest once it establishes dominance. To lessen the chances that bears will disrupt your campsite, suspend with a rope all food, garbage, and scented products from a downwind and distant tree (a minimum of 10 feet above the ground, 10 feet from the trunk, and 5 feet from the branch). Leave no food scraps around the camp and be sure that no scent of food stays on your body or clothes.

Mountain lions. Most hikers go their entire lives without spotting even one of these large predators, and for good reason: Mountain lions require a lot of territory per lion, and they usually avoid humans. However, lion attacks on humans have increased recently, although the odds of this happening to you are extremely low. To keep those odds as low as possible, don't hike alone and do leave the dog at home (it can attract lions). If a lion does approach you, pick up any small children. In contrast to the advice regarding bears, you should hold your ground, extend your arms to look as large as possible, throw rocks, and shout. Do NOT crouch or turn your back on the lion. If you're attacked, fight back.

Horses. You'll occasionally meet horseback riders on the trail. Step aside and speak calmly with the riders to let the horses know that they needn't fear you.

Hikers must often share the trail with horseback riders.

Poison oak. This plant grows at elevations as high as 5,000 feet and can take a variety of confusing disguises ranging from small shrub to snaky vine. An important part of the subterfuge is leaf shape, which varies from plant to plant. The telltale sign of poison oak (actually, for what could be poison oak) is a cluster of three leaves. Some people develop an itchy, red rash after contact with poison oak. If you think you touched poison oak, or touched someone or something that touched poison oak, wash immediately with soap and cool water (also wash the clothes you're wearing). Many stores sell products that help suppress the symptoms.

A Note About Safety

Safety is an important concern in all outdoor activities. No guidebook can alert you to every hazard or anticipate the limitations of every reader. Therefore, the descriptions of roads, trails, routes, and natural features in this book are not representations that a particular place or excursion will be safe for your party. When you follow any of the routes described in this book, you assume responsibility for your own safety. Under normal conditions, such excursions require the usual attention to traffic, road and trail conditions, weather, terrain, the capabilities of your party, and other factors. Keeping informed about current conditions and exercising common sense are the keys to a safe, enjoyable outing.

The Mountaineers

Wilderness Ethics

The philosophy of minimum impact is your guide. It requires that you seek to leave no trace of your passage through the wild.

Walking. Do not shortcut up or down trail switchbacks. Step on firm ground or rocks. When in meadows (which have especially sensitive plants), be as careful as possible.

Camping. Choose a spot at least 100 feet away from lakes, rivers, and streams to ensure that you don't disturb riparian habitat or pollute the water. Use existing sites when possible, preferably those on bare rock or in open forest. Place a plastic tarp under your tent to exclude rainwater; don't dig trenches.

Fires. Learn to be happy and warm without them. Fires scare away animals, pollute the atmosphere, and remove important organic and inorganic materials from the local ecosystem. Bring extra clothes for warmth and cook with a gas stove. A wide variety of foods need no cooking at all, and "caffiends" can pop caffeine pills in the morning, eliminating the need for a stove. If you must indulge in a campfire (in an established ring only), have it in or near a heavily wooded area, use only dead wood that's fallen on the ground, and thoroughly douse it with water when done.

Washing. Protect aquatic life by keeping food particles and detergents out of lakes, rivers, and streams. Buy biodegradable soaps (sold at outdoor stores) and wash over bare rock or far back in the woods.

Garbage. Pack it all out.

Sanitation. Travel a minimum of 200 feet away from water and far from trails and campsites to defecate. Dig a hole 6 to 10 inches deep, preferably in forest duff, where the feces will decompose relatively rapidly. Stay away from water sources, camps, and trails when you urinate, and spread it around the ground so it'll enrich the soil with nitrogen.

Courtesy. Be as unobtrusive as possible: Speak quietly; travel in small groups; select subdued earth colors such as green, gray, and brown for your clothes and equipment; choose an inconspicuous campsite. And don't bring your dog; dogs scare away wildlife, pollute water, occasionally threaten other hikers, and can attract mountain lions.

Enjoying the Wilderness

When you enter the wild, open your senses to the sights, sounds, smells, and feel of your surroundings. Mosey along and stop often: The journey itself is what's most important, not reaching a mountaintop or completing an entire hike. It's better to saunter a slow mile with heightened senses and a calm soul than to rush through the hike on a workday schedule.

Butterflies add grace and beauty to any surrounding.

LEGEND

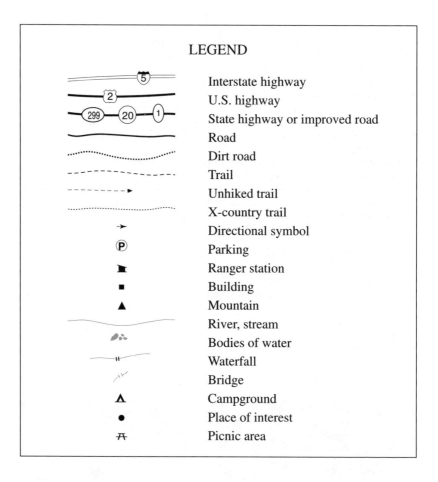

	Interstate highway
	U.S. highway
	State highway or improved road
	Road
	Dirt road
	Trail
	Unhiked trail
	X-country trail
	Directional symbol
	Parking
	Ranger station
	Building
	Mountain
	River, stream
	Bodies of water
	Waterfall
	Bridge
	Campground
	Place of interest
	Picnic area

LASSEN VOLCANIC NATIONAL PARK

Chaos Crags stretch high above the shoreline of Crags Lake.

⌶ BROKEOFF MOUNTAIN

Length: 7 miles round trip
Hiking time: 5 hours or 2 days
High point: 9,235 feet
Total elevation gain: 2,550 feet
Difficulty: strenuous
Season: mid-July through October
Water: available only the first two miles; purify first; you'll need a lot
Maps: USGS 7.5' Lassen Peak, park brochure
Permit: required for overnight trips; obtain from the Loomis Museum at the park's northwest entrance station, from the park's Mineral office, or from the Almanor Ranger District in Chester
Nearest campground: Southwest Campground
Information: Lassen Volcanic National Park

The view from Brokeoff's summit rivals that of the more famous (and much more visited) Lassen Peak 3 miles to the northeast. But the Brokeoff Mountain trail offers many attractions lacking on the Lassen Peak trail—creeks, ponds, a lake, shady forest, a wide variety of wildflowers, and permission to backpack (backpackers should look for level areas from a half mile in to the vicinity of Forest Lake). Check the

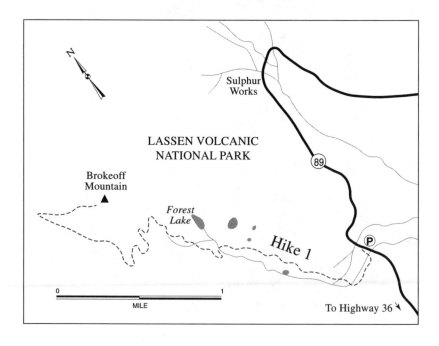

The view north from Brokeoff Mountain summit: remnants of Mount Tehama lead to Lassen Peak (Photo by Marc J. Soares)

weather forecast for thunderstorms and read the relevant precautions for these potentially dangerous events in the **Weather** section in the *Introduction*.

The trail begins at post 2 on Highway 89's west side, 5 miles north of the junctions of Highways 36 and 89, and 29 miles south of the junctions of Highways 44 and 89.

The path first crosses a Mill Creek feeder stream that's lined with willows and mountain alders, then enters a forest of lodgepole pine, western white pine, and red fir. It travels just above a trailside pond at 0.8 mile and then climbs past a series of moist meadows vibrant with summer wildflowers.

At 1.3 miles, you'll cross a small stream. If you follow it uphill for 250 yards, you'll reach tree-ringed Forest Lake, a pleasant side trip.

The ascent then steepens and enters more open territory, offering far-reaching views that increase in scope as you gain elevation. The trail winds along the south flanks of Brokeoff, with the gradient moderating as you close in on the summit. At this high elevation, few plants can survive the frigid winter temperatures and whipping winds: Look for a few weather-stunted mountain hemlocks and whitebark pines.

Reaching the final destination, the park's second highest peak at 9,235 feet, is cause for celebration. After calming your heart, breathe in the stunning panorama. Your immediate surroundings comprise the remains of ancient Mount Tehama, the most prominent remnants being Brokeoff itself; the ridge stretching northeast that's topped by Mount Diller, Pilot Pinnacle, and Eagle Peak; Mount Conard 3 miles southeast; and Sulphur Works far below, probably the volcano's vent. This massive volcano once soared to 11,000 feet before a combination of glaciation, internal collapse, and possibly collapse along a fault brought about its demise.

Many other landmarks vie for your attention. Lassen Peak and distant Mount Shasta lie to the north. The entire realm of Lassen Park stretches east, with Lake Almanor leading to the Sierra Nevada to the south. The Sacramento Valley lies west, with the Coast Range and Klamath Mountains beyond.

2 MILL CREEK FALLS

Length: 3.2 miles round trip
Hiking time: 2 hours, day hike only
High point: 6,750 feet
Total elevation gain: 350 feet
Difficulty: moderate
Season: mid-June through late October
Water: bring your own
Maps: USGS 7.5' Lassen Peak, park brochure
Permit: none required
Nearest campground: Southwest Campground
Information: Lassen Volcanic National Park

East Sulphur Creek and the stream draining Bumpass Hell approach each other at the lip of Mill Creek Falls, where they separately plunge 30 feet to meet at a small pool, then intertwine and drop another 50 feet into a large pool. This is an auspicious beginning to Mill Creek, a major northern California stream that leaves the park and flows southwest through the steep canyons of the Ishi Wilderness to merge with the Sacramento River.

Reach Southwest Campground, which is on Highway 89's east side, 6 miles north of the junction of Highways 36 and 89, and 28 miles southeast of the junction of Highways 44 and 89. The trail begins from the north side of the campground by site 19.

Descend 0.3 mile through a forest of small red firs and a few lodgepole pines to reach West Sulphur Creek, a stream laden with minerals from Sulphur Works a mile upstream. Stop midway as you cross the wooden bridge for a close-up examination of mountain alder.

Once on the other side, climb through an open area where mule ears

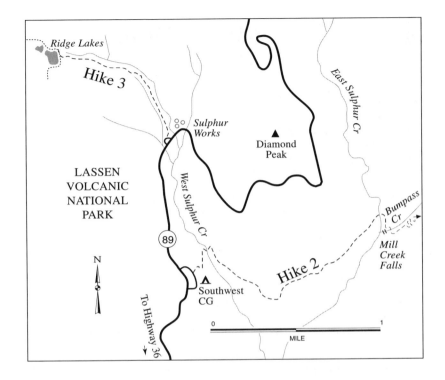

flourish and several large western white pines reach heights and long cone lengths that rival the splendor of their lower elevation cousin, the sugar pine.

From here, the trail undulates eastward all the way to the falls overlook. Red firs, white firs, and western white pines provide some shade for you and an understory of currants and flowers. Look behind for occasional views of Brokeoff Mountain and Mount Diller; you'll also catch glimpses of Mount Conard to the south and Diamond Peak to the north.

The roar of the falls rises in your ears at 1.5 miles, followed soon by the vista point at 1.6 miles. From near the edge of the cliff, you'll see the entire length of the falls and the bordering rock cliffs that are stained brownish red and adorned with green moss. Photographers will want to be here from late morning through mid-afternoon; all water lovers will want to come early and stay late.

If you desire more hiking, continue on the trail above the top of the falls. The path travels 1.8 miles past lush Conard Meadows to Crumbaugh Lake, where you can head to the Kings Creek Picnic Area (hike 7) or Bumpass Hell (hike 4).

3
SULPHUR WORKS
AND RIDGE LAKES

Length: 2.2 miles round trip
Hiking time: 2 hours or 2 days
High point: 8,000 feet
Total elevation gain: 1,000 feet
Difficulty: moderate to strenuous
Season: early July through mid-October
Water: available from creeks and at Ridge Lakes; purify first
Maps: USGS 7.5' Lassen Peak, park brochure
Permit: required for overnight trips; obtain from the Loomis Museum at the park's northwest entrance station, from the park's Mineral office, or from the Almanor Ranger District in Chester
Nearest campground: Southwest Campground
Information: Lassen Volcanic National Park

Map on page 23

Start this hike with a tour of geothermal theatrics at Sulphur Works, then climb a mile up a steep trail to win the isolation of the Ridge Lakes, where chilly swimming, good views, and cross-country hiking await.

Drive to the Sulphur Works parking lot, which is on Highway 89's west side, 7 miles north of the junction of Highways 36 and 89, and 27 miles southeast of the junction of Highways 44 and 89.

Follow the acrid scent of hydrogen sulfide over to the Sulphur Works. Here a boardwalk and informational signs guide you past the mud pots, fumaroles, and steam jets of Mount Tehama's central vent; cool surface water descends to hot magma far below, then rises as hot water and steam around you. When Mount Tehama rose to an estimated elevation of 11,000 feet, it held undisputed bragging rights as the biggest volcano south of Mount Shasta. Alas, volcanoes on its flanks drained off lava, leading to a collapse of the central portions of the mountain. Ice-age glaciation did most of the later destruction; Brokeoff Mountain, rising to a height of 9,235 feet due west, is the highest remaining fragment of Mount Tehama.

Return to the north side of the parking lot and begin the Ridge Lakes trail. The steep path heads up a ridge between two forks of West Sulphur Creek all the way to the lakes. At the beginning, you quickly reach the crest, where coyote mint, lupines, mule ears, and ferns grow in abundance, and from which you can gaze down upon Sulphur Works. As you continue, you'll spy Brokeoff Mountain. On the probably frequent stops to lower your pulse rate, look behind for views of the Sierra Nevada, the Mill Creek drainage, and southern Lassen Park landmarks.

You soon weave in and out of forest shade provided by red firs and western white pines, then spy a side trail to the right at 0.3 mile that passes through a mountain alder thicket to a creek fork. The main path soon reenters a flower-strewn open area, then continues relentlessly up. Mountain hemlocks provide welcome company as you persevere. A glimpse north at the sharp slant of Mount Diller will make you grateful that the path isn't any steeper than it is.

The Ridge Lakes await in a glacial cirque 1 mile from the trail's beginning. Here you have a vista that includes Brokeoff Mountain and Mount Diller, plus the ridge that stretches between them. Brave swimmers will want to enter at the deepest section of the southern lake (the two are joined until late summer), and campers will find sheltered spots amid red fir and mountain mahogany on the northeast side of the lakes.

Consider two easy cross-country options. The first involves circling to the southwest side of the lake and climbing briefly through a lupine field to a low gap. The second takes you up a gully on the northwest side, where you'll gain an easy 300 feet of elevation as you ascend to a ridge. From here you'll have a north and west panorama that runs from Mount Shasta to the Klamath Mountains, Coast Range, and Sacramento Valley; you'll also see the southern portion of Lassen Park.

The Ridge Lakes and Mount Diller

4

LAKE HELEN TO BUMPASS HELL

Length: 3 miles round trip
Hiking time: 2 hours, day hike only
High point: 8,400 feet
Total elevation gain: 450 feet
Difficulty: moderate
Season: early July through late October
Water: none; bring your own
Maps: USGS 7.5' Lassen Peak, park brochure
Permit: none required
Nearest campground: Southwest Campground
Information: Lassen Volcanic National Park

This hike is one of Lassen Park's most popular, and justifiably so. It's an easy 1.5-mile stroll that features trailside snowbanks through mid-August for children to play in; beautiful blue lupines and a mosaic of other colorful flowers; panoramic views of Lassen Peak, Brokeoff Mountain, and other prominent geographic features; and close-up examination of Bumpass Hell, where bubbling mud pots, steaming fumaroles, and large boiling pools provide ample evidence of the hot magma still seething far below the surface. A brochure available at the trailhead provides extensive information about trailside ecology and geology, with a special focus on Bumpass Hell (it's keyed to numbered

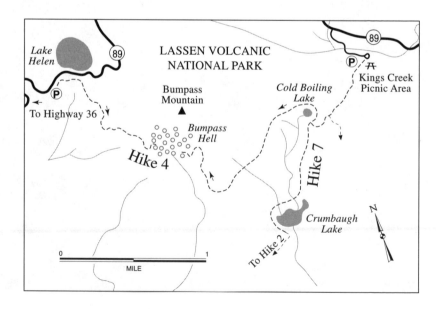

A boardwalk makes it easy to examine Bumpass Hell's geothermal activity

posts). Note that it's easy to hike all the way to Kings Creek Picnic Area (4.0 miles total) by tacking on hike 7 and arranging to be picked up at its trailhead.

The adventure begins from the large lot at post 17 on Highway 89, about 11 miles north of the junction of Highways 36 and 89, and 23 miles southeast of the junction of Highways 44 and 89.

The path initially parallels the road and allows excellent views of Lassen Peak, then climbs to run fairly level in a southwesterly direction. You'll find the best vista point near number 13 of the nature brochure. Brokeoff Mountain dominates to the west, with the Coast Range rising far beyond, above the Sacramento Valley. Mount Conard lies due south, as does the long chain of the Sierra Nevada.

The trail soon descends to Bumpass Hell, a 16-acre depression of surreal nightmare named for discoverer Kendall Vanhook Bumpass, who lost a leg after stepping in one of the thermal pools. Avoid the same fate (or worse) by staying on the boardwalk as you explore, and keep a close eye on children.

A vast mass of hot magma miles below boils water to steam, which then surges up through cracks and fissures to emerge here to create the bubbling pools, fumaroles, and mud pots. The smell of rotten eggs comes from hydrogen sulfide in the steam. Sulfuric acid, other chemicals, and the hot steam have combined to decompose much of the rock here and create a kaleidoscope of yellow, red, and brown.

Upon your return to the trailhead, consider a picnic at Lake Helen across the road. The gorgeous and deep glacial lake provides a perfect backdrop for unimpeded views of Lassen Peak.

Nearby: Extend your trek by continuing eastward from Bumpass Hell with hike 7, which also allows you to travel to Mill Creek Falls (hike 2).

5 LASSEN PEAK

Length: 5 miles round trip
Hiking time: 4 hours, day hike only
High point: 10,453 feet
Total elevation gain: 2,000 feet
Difficulty: moderate to strenuous
Season: mid-July through October
Water: none; bring at least 1 quart per person
Maps: USGS 7.5' Lassen Peak, park brochure
Permit: none required
Nearest campground: Southwest Campground
Information: Lassen Volcanic National Park

Lassen Peak, a volcano spectacularly active in the early twentieth century, looms large in northern California, dominating Lassen Park and surrounding terrain. Visible for more than a hundred miles in every direction, it tempts all hikers to climb the winding path up barren slopes to gain the summit and unparalleled views. You'll need some physical conditioning to succeed: The air thins at this high elevation, and the trail has a fairly steep gradient. You'll also need to prepare for cold temperatures, high winds, and strong sun, and don't start the climb if thunderstorms threaten (see the **Weather** section in the *Introduction* for precautions).

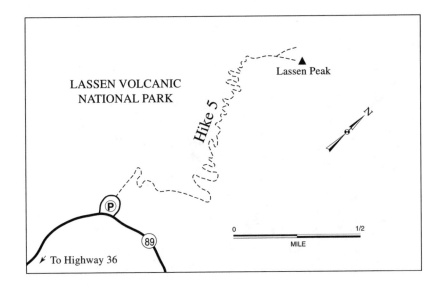

The spacious trailhead parking area is 12 miles north of the junction of Highways 36 and 89, and 22 miles southeast of the junction of Highways 44 and 89.

The route begins at the north side of the parking lot, where you'll find nature brochures for the trail. You quickly reach a grove of mountain hemlocks, then, a bit farther up, some whitebark pines. The twisted and battered shapes of the latter give silent testimony to the harsh winds and temperatures that prevail here in winter.

The path then ascends at a steady rate up an open slope that provides an anchor for only a few alpine wildflowers but gives far-ranging vistas when you stop to catch your breath. However, let the surety of even better views pull you to the top.

From the rim of Lassen Peak, elevation 10,453 feet, you'll see all the major Lassen Park landmarks, including Chaos Crags, Prospect Peak, Mount Harkness, Reading Peak, and Brokeoff Mountain. The Warner Mountains and the Modoc Plateau fill out the far northeastern and eastern vista. To the south, you'll see Lake Almanor and the spine of the northern Sierra Nevada. The Sacramento Valley and the Coast Range lie to the west, while the Klamath Mountains claim the northwest. Crater and Magee peaks and Burney Mountain rise to the near north, with mighty Mount Shasta anchoring the far horizon.

Lassen Peak, a plug-dome volcano, formed from a vent on the northern edge of ancient Mount Tehama about 25,000 years ago when large volumes of thick, pasty dacite were extruded over a period of several years. Modern volcanic activity began in May 1914 with ash and steam eruptions, soon escalating to eruptions of lava chunks. In May 1915, lava rose in the crater and spilled over the west and northeast sides;

29

Lassen Peak as viewed from the summit of Brokeoff Mountain (Photo by Marc J. Soares)

the northeast flow melted snow that flooded Hat Creek and Lost Creek. A few days later, Lassen ejected an ash cloud 25,000 feet in the air and shot a lateral blast of magma down the path of the northeast lava flow, knocking over trees and completing the formation of the Devastated Area. Through 1917, the mountain ejected more chunks of lava; minor steam eruptions continued until 1921.

6 TERRACE, SHADOW, AND CLIFF LAKES

Length: 3.4 miles round trip
Hiking time: 2 hours, day hike only
High point: 8,050 feet
Total elevation gain: 700 feet
Difficulty: easy to moderate
Season: early July through late October
Water: available from the lakes; purify first
Maps: USGS 7.5' Reading Peak, park brochure
Permit: none required
Nearest campground: Summit Lake Campground
Information: Lassen Volcanic National Park

This hike offers an easy way to reach three gorgeous lakes. It's popular with families and those wanting a short jaunt to Terrace Lake. If you desire more solitude, journey past Terrace and Shadow lakes to Cliff Lake. You also have two options for one-way car shuttle trips: The first takes you to Hat Lake; the second takes you to Dersch Meadows and the Summit Lake Ranger Station.

The trail begins at road post 27 on Highway 89's north side, 14 miles northeast of the junction of Highways 36 and 89, and 20 miles southeast of the junction of Highways 44 and 89.

Begin a moderate descent through a forest dominated by mountain hemlock, then reach a trail fork at 0.2 mile. Hike 11 heads downhill to Paradise Meadows and Hat Lake and offers the opportunity for a

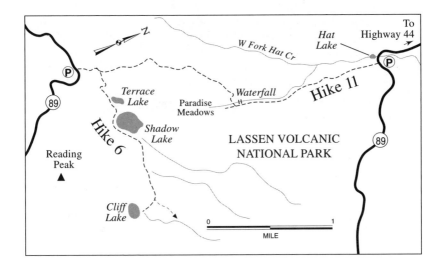

A young red fir graces the shoreline of Shadow Lake.

one-way trip (have someone pick you up at the hike 11 trailhead at road post 42).

For now, go right and continue the descent to Terrace Lake at 0.5 mile. Swimmers will find a grassy beach with a gentle slope into the water on the south side; however, as with the other two lakes, the temperature doesn't climb to pleasant levels until August.

The path soon drops to Shadow Lake, which is ringed by a diverse forest of mountain hemlocks, red firs, lodgepole pines, and western white pines. As you curve around the lake's east side, look for Lassen Peak reflected on the sapphire-blue surface.

From Shadow Lake, you'll head east and gently downward. Look for small ponds on the left at 1.3 miles, then glance behind for another view of Lassen Peak.

A trail runs right (south) at 1.5 miles. Take it 0.2 mile to its end near the outlet stream of Cliff Lake. Reading Peak, a plug-dome volcano like Lassen Peak and Chaos Crags, rises abruptly just to the south to an elevation of 8,701 feet. Its steep, talus-tumble flanks meet the water's edge and give the lake its name. Cliff Lake, which harbors a small island topped by mountain hemlocks and red firs, is the best of the three lakes for exploration and a picnic.

Your second one-way car shuttle option leaves from the trail fork 0.2 mile from Cliff Lake. The path travels 2.4 miles down through open forest to meet Highway 89 and Dersch Meadows at road post 38. From here, it's a 0.2 mile walk to the Summit Lake Ranger Station (road post 37), the best place to meet your ride.

7 COLD BOILING LAKE, CRUMBAUGH LAKE, AND BUMPASS HELL

Length: 6 miles round trip
Hiking time: 4 hours, day hike only
High point: 8,350 feet
Total elevation gain: 1,500 feet
Difficulty: moderate
Season: late June through October
Water: available only at Crumbaugh Lake; purify first
Maps: USGS 7.5' Reading Peak, USGS 7.5' Lassen Peak, park brochure
Permit: none required
Nearest campground: Summit Lake Campground
Information: Lassen Volcanic National Park

Map on page 26

This hike lets you take the path less traveled by to Bumpass Hell, thus allowing you to avoid the crowds that throng the trail that begins near Lake Helen and is described in hike 4. (You can do a one-way trip by arranging to be picked up at the hike 4 trailhead, although you'll do a lot less climbing if you begin with hike 4 and end with this one.) This journey also takes you to Cold Boiling Lake and Crumbaugh Lake; the latter receives few visitors and attracts hikers who like solitude and beautiful scenery. For another one-way trip, hike

A hiker stops to inspect Cold Boiling Lake.

past Crumbaugh Lake to Mill Creek Falls and the trails of hike 2.

Travel Highway 89 to road post 30, which is 16.5 miles northeast of the junction of Highways 36 and 89, and 17.5 miles southeast of the junction of Highways 44 and 89. Take the side road 0.3 mile down to the trailhead at Kings Creek Picnic Area.

Find the trail at the south side of the parking lot. It begins with a brisk but brief ascent, then travels a level stretch past red firs, mountain hemlocks, and lodgepole pines. Bear right at a trail fork at 0.5 mile and continue 0.2 mile to Cold Boiling Lake, where gas from deep underground rises to make bubbles at the water's surface.

You'll also find a trail fork here. Bumpass Hell lies uphill to the right. But for now, head left and descend 0.5 mile past a green meadow decorated with corn lily and red mountain heather to Crumbaugh Lake. From the lake's shore you have an excellent southward view of Mount Conard's 8,204-foot summit. It's another 2.2 miles to Mill Creek Falls and hike 2.

To go to Bumpass Hell, return to Cold Boiling Lake and start a 1.8-mile westerly climb that features views of Mount Conard, Crumbaugh Lake, Cold Boiling Lake, and Bumpass Mountain. Along the way, you'll cross two small streams and reach a saddle just above Bumpass Hell.

The hydrothermal theatrics at Bumpass Hell highlight this trip. Groundwater seeps deep underground to a chamber of hot magma where it heats up and rises to the surface. Look for the resulting fumaroles, mud pots, and steam vents as you traverse the nearly barren landscape on the wooden boardwalk. The boardwalk is here for your protection; the hot water can cause severe burns.

8 KINGS CREEK, KINGS CREEK FALLS, AND SIFFORD LAKES

Length: 5.3 miles round trip
Hiking time: 4 hours or 2 days
High point: 7,200 feet
Total elevation gain: 500 feet
Difficulty: easy to moderate
Season: late June through October
Water: available from Kings Creek and Sifford Lakes; purify first
Maps: USGS 7.5' Reading Peak, park brochure
Permit: required for overnight trips; obtain from the Loomis Museum at the park's northwest entrance station, from the park's Mineral office, or from the Almanor Ranger District in Chester
Nearest campground: Summit Lake Campground
Information: Lassen Volcanic National Park

Kings Creek begins near Lassen Peak's southern flanks and flows down through Warner Valley to join the North Fork Feather River. This walk first takes you along the stream's prettiest section to magnificent Kings Creek Falls, then journeys up to the Sifford Lakes, where several shallow lakes offer isolation, good swimming, and campsites for backpackers.

Take Highway 89 to road post 32, which is 17 miles northeast of the junction of Highways 36 and 89, and 17 miles southeast of the junction

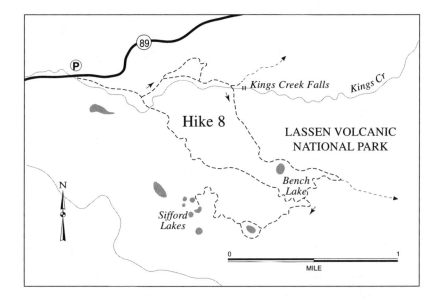

of Highways 44 and 89. Park in the lot on the north side of Highway 89.

The trail starts on the south side of the road. It borders the lush meadow that cradles Kings Creek and occasionally dips into a forest of red fir, mountain hemlock, western white pine, and lodgepole pine. Head left at a trail fork at 0.4 mile (you'll return via the right fork), then go right at another fork at 0.6 mile (the left-hand trail is a gentler, less dangerous route to the falls).

Multi-tiered Kings Creek Falls

You now walk on rocky ledges near the creek's tumbling cascades, an area that requires careful attention to footing. The way soon levels, then meets at 1 mile the trail you'll take to the Sifford Lakes. Make a mental note of it, then continue left for the final 100 yards to the lip of Kings Creek Falls, where the water leaves lush greenery to leap 50 feet to the hard rocks below. You also need to watch your step near the edge of the canyon. If you want a picture of the falls in full sunlight, arrive here in late morning.

When you're relaxed and ready, head back to the last trail fork, cross Kings Creek, and begin the journey to the Sifford Lakes. The path ascends steeply, but soon the gradient moderates as you pass under a talus cliff with two small caves near the top. Bench Lake appears 0.6 mile from Kings Creek; its shallow waters usually dry up by late summer.

Continue the climb, bearing right at a trail fork 0.4 mile farther, then left at another trail fork 0.3 mile farther. From here, it's 0.4 mile to the first Sifford Lake, where you'll find a good opportunity to swim the relatively warm waters and a good campsite near the north shore. A faint path runs northwest to the next Sifford Lake, which boasts two campsites, better swimming, and even more privacy. You can explore the other nearby Sifford Lakes by traveling cross-country.

When it's time to return, head back to the trail fork 0.4 mile below the first Sifford Lake. Go left and ramble downhill 0.9 mile to a crossing of Kings Creek, after which you turn left for the last 0.4 mile to the trailhead.

9 TWIN LAKES, SNAG LAKE, AND HORSESHOE LAKE

Length: 17.6-mile loop
Hiking time: 2 to 3 days
High point: 7,100 feet
Total elevation gain: 2,100 feet
Difficulty: moderate
Season: mid-June through October
Water: available from lakes and streams; purify first
Maps: USGS 7.5' Reading Peak, USGS 7.5' West Prospect Peak, USGS 7.5' Prospect Peak, USGS 7.5' Mount Harkness, park brochure
Permit: required for overnight trips; obtain from the Loomis Museum at the park's northwest entrance station, from the park's Mineral office, or from the Almanor Ranger District in Chester
Nearest campground: Summit Lake Campground
Information: Lassen Volcanic National Park

This hike loops through the heart of Lassen Park and travels some of its most beautiful country. You'll walk through miles of open pine/fir forest, visit a half dozen of the park's biggest lakes, and have views of all the park's major volcanoes. For those desiring an extended trek, it's easy

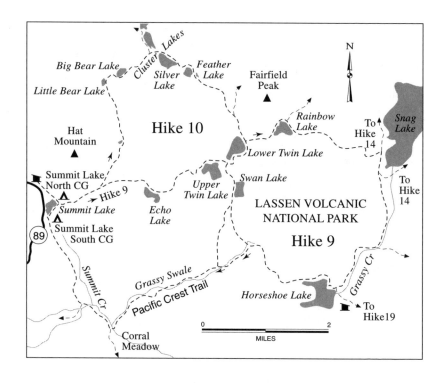

to join up with hikes 14, 17, 19, 20, and 21, which travel to the far northern, southern, and eastern edges of the park and even to the Caribou Wilderness, home of hikes 22 through 25. Leaving from Summit Lake is the most convenient way to enter the Lassen Park backcountry because of easy access off Highway 89. If desired, arrange a car shuttle to pick you up at a trailhead for any of the just-mentioned hikes.

The hike starts 100 yards east of the day-use parking area at the Summit Lake North Campground, which is on Highway 89's east side, 20.5 miles northeast of the junction of Highways 36 and 89, and 13.5 miles southeast of the junctions of Highways 44 and 89. Backpackers must park their vehicles 0.3 mile north of the campground at the ranger station. A short path leads from the ranger station to the hike's beginning.

Start along the edge of Summit Lake; the water's surface presents shimmering images of Lassen Peak, which rises to the west, and Reading Peak, prominent to the southwest. A trail fork, the hike's official start, awaits on the lake's east side. The right fork serves as the return trail for the loop, but begin by heading left.

The path climbs past red firs, western white pines, and mountain hemlocks, the dominant trees of the elevation range of this trip (you'll also see numerous lodgepole pines near lake shores and bordering

Grassy Swale). The trees occasionally part to give a different perspective on Lassen Peak and Reading Peak.

Another trail fork awaits at 0.9 mile. Hike 10 runs to the left; you go right, past chaparral, descending gradually to Echo Lake at 1.7 miles. Echo Lake ranks as one of the most beautiful lakes anywhere. Alas, you eventually will have to move on because camping is forbidden at or near this lake (you can camp at all the other lakes encountered on this hike).

Climb briefly, then descend gently past two ponds to reach large and deep Upper Twin Lake at 3.1 miles. Walk along the north shore past several campsites, bear left at a trail fork onto the Pacific Crest Trail (a right provides a shortcut to Horsehoe Lake and Corral Meadow), then reach Lower Twin Lake. Note the views of Prospect Peak to the north as you swing around the south shore near several more campsites.

On the east side of the lake at 4.3 miles, you'll find a trail fork. Go right, climb briefly, run level, then descend to Rainbow Lake at 4.8 miles. This lake, nestled next to Fairfield Peak, features good swimming and campsites near the west and east shores.

Bear right at a fork near the northeast shore (a left leads 2.2 miles to hike 14 near Cinder Cone). The way climbs briefly, then loses 600 feet of elevation as it drops down to Snag Lake and another junction at

The view of Lassen Peak from the shore of Summit Lake

7.0 miles, where you briefly join hike 14. Snag Lake, the park's second largest, offers several campsites in the vicinity, along with good views of surrounding terrain.

Head right 0.5 mile to where, after 0.4 mile, an east-branching trail would bring you to hike 21. Head right again and begin a gentle ascent that takes you along the lush banks of Grassy Creek (stay right at the fork) to Horseshoe Lake and another fork at 9.7 miles. Horseshoe Lake has views of both Mount Harkness and Lassen Peak and offers a large number of campsites, especially on the east side (you can do hikes 17, 19, and 20 from here also).

Go right and travel a level 1.4 miles along the north shore, then beyond the shore another 1.4 miles to a fork. Bear left and then left again, as you rejoin the Pacific Crest Trail for a downhill ramble through Grassy Swale. Grassy Swale has lush meadows bursting with flowers and level areas sheltered by lodgepole pines that make good campsites.

Reach Kings Creek and several campsites at Corral Meadow at 14.9 miles. Bear right at a trail fork and head north near Summit Creek. Go right again at another fork, then continue to the southern edge of Summit Lake, where a path takes you to the northern shore and the hike's starting point at 17.6 miles.

10 CLUSTER LAKES AND TWIN LAKES

Length: 10.8 miles round trip
Hiking time: 7 hours or 2 days
High point: 7,300 feet
Total elevation gain: 1,000 feet
Difficulty: moderate
Season: mid-June through October
Water: available from lakes; purify first
Maps: USGS 7.5' Reading Peak, USGS 7.5' West Prospect Peak, USGS 7.5' Prospect Peak, park brochure
Permit: required for overnight trips; obtain from the Loomis Museum at the park's northwest entrance station, from the park's Mineral office, or from the Almanor Ranger District in Chester
Nearest campground: Summit Lake Campground
Information: Lassen Volcanic National Park

Map on page 38

This popular trip features lakes, lakes, lakes. You'll visit no less than nine major bodies of water, including many of Lassen Park's prettiest. As an added bonus, you'll have views of Lassen Peak, Reading Peak, and Prospect Peak thrown into the bargain. Backpackers will find plenty of sites at which to sleep, while day hikers will receive a

The driftwood-littered shoreline of one of the Cluster lakes

moderate stamina challenge. This trip also allows you to connect with hike 9 and thus continue to the far reaches of Lassen Park and, through other hikes, beyond to the Caribou Wilderness.

The trail begins 100 yards east of the day-use parking area at the Summit Lake North Campground, which is on Highway 89's east side, 20.5 miles northeast of the junction of Highways 36 and 89, and 13.5 miles southeast of the junctions of Highways 44 and 89. Backpackers must park 0.3 mile north of the campground at the ranger station, where a short trail brings them to the beginning of the hike.

The way initially hugs the shoreline of Summit Lake, which gives a stunning view of Lassen Peak and Reading Peak. You'll quickly reach a trail fork: Bear left and head uphill through a forest of western white pine, red fir, and mountain hemlock. These trees will be with you for all of the forested journey, though you'll also note numerous lodgepole pines ringing lake shores.

Enjoy more views of Lassen Peak and Reading Peak, then reach another trail fork at 0.9 mile. Hike 9 goes right, but bear left, noting that you'll return via the right-hand trail.

You'll soon finish climbing to run fairly level as Hat Mountain appears a mile to the west. Swing around the north side of a pond, then make a long and gentle descent that gives northward views of Prospect Peak and West Prospect Peak, in addition to Magee Peak and other Thousand Lakes Wilderness summits.

Little Bear Lake awaits at 3.3 miles. Like many lakes in Lassen Park, its level drops as summer progresses. Flat areas for camping lie on the south side, but you'd do just as well to push on to Big Bear Lake at 3.6 miles; it offers level sites on its southwest side and has deeper water for swimmers.

Descend to a trail fork at 4.2 miles. A brief jaunt left brings you to one of the Cluster Lakes, where turpentine-scented Labrador tea grows profusely on the west bank—a good spot to admire the ridge rising 500 feet above the water on the east side.

The hike heads right to skirt past level camping areas and soon borders large and shallow Silver Lake. Continue to deeper Feather Lake at 4.8 miles; you'll find flat camping spots between the lake and a pond on the left side of the trail.

The path passes another pond as it heads slightly downslope, then reaches a junction with the Pacific Crest Trail at 6.2 miles. Note Fairfield Peak rising just to the east, then push on for 0.2 mile to the shores of Lower Twin Lake, which features many campsites and great swimming. Another fork awaits on the lake's east shore, where you join up with hike 9.

To continue back to the trailhead, go right and then right again at another fork on the southwest edge of Lower Twin Lake. The way quickly leads to Upper Twin Lake, which rivals its sister in size and beauty and has several campsites near the trail.

Climb up past two ponds, then reach beautiful Echo Lake (no camping allowed) where forested ridges surround the deep, clear water on all four sides. From here, it's 1.8 miles to the previously encountered trail fork and another mile down to the campground and day-use parking area.

11 TERRACE, SHADOW, AND CLIFF LAKES VIA PARADISE MEADOWS

Length: 8.4 miles round trip
Hiking time: 5 hours, day hike only
High point: 7,800 feet
Total elevation gain: 1,800 feet
Difficulty: moderate
Season: early July through late October
Water: available from streams and lakes; purify first
Maps: USGS 7.5' West Prospect Peak, USGS 7.5' Reading Peak, park brochure
Permit: none required
Nearest campground: Summit Lake Campground
Information: Lassen Volcanic National Park

Map on page 31

This hike takes you the back way to Terrace, Shadow, and Cliff lakes, a route that features serene stretches of virgin forest, perennial streams, a 20-foot waterfall, a gorgeous meadow overflowing with wildflowers, and excellent views of Lassen Peak. It's easy to combine it with hike 6 for a one-way trip, but you'd probably want to begin with hike 6 and arrange to be picked up at this hike's trailhead so that you can walk down instead of up.

Park in the lot at road post 42, which is 24 miles north of the junction of Highways 36 and 89, and 10 miles southeast of the junction of Highways 44 and 89.

The hike begins on the south side of Highway 89. You'll initially pass just east of Hat Lake. In May 1915, Lassen Peak erupted, sending hot lava down her northeast flanks. The lava melted snow and mixed with dirt to form mud, which spilled down to dam Hat Creek and form the lake. Hat Lake was once much larger, but it has quickly

Waterfall below Paradise Meadows

filled with sediments. Today, it's only a small pond.

The trail initially runs fairly level and offers an occasional glimpse of Lassen Peak. It then begins a long and relatively steep climb through a forest of western white pine, red fir, and mountain hemlock. Look for yellow lupines early on and blue lupines farther up. You almost always will be within sight and sound of the West Fork Hat Creek or a tributary.

At 1.3 miles, a 20-foot waterfall tumbles over several rock ledges, an indicator of even more beauty to come. Reach a trail fork just beyond the waterfall and continue straight 100 yards to reach the edge of Paradise Meadows. This vast, open expanse especially deserves its name in August when a wildflower bonanza bursts forth from the lush greenery. A small stream leisurely glides through the center of the meadows, and Reading Peak stands guard to the south.

When the meadow has thoroughly mellowed you, return to the trail fork, cross the creek, and begin climbing, initially past red fir and western white pine. Farther up, mountain hemlocks join the forest, but all the trees occasionally part to give clear views of Lassen Peak rising high 2 miles to the west.

Reach a trail fork at 2.7 miles. A right turn will lead you up 0.2 mile to road post 27 at Highway 89, the trailhead for hike 6. For a discussion of the rest of the route to Terrace, Shadow, and Cliff Lakes, see hike 6.

Nearby: For more hiking, head east 0.2 mile from the trailhead to post 41 and the Nobles Emigrant Trail. This long path runs north to connect with the Pacific Crest Trail. Also consider a visit to post 43, located 0.4 mile to the northwest of Hat Lake; at the large parking lot, you can read about the eruption that created the Devastated Area in 1915, then look directly ahead for visual proof on the slopes of nearby Lassen Peak. A short, paved trail takes you past several more signs that detail the eruption and its aftermath.

12 CHAOS CRAGS AND CRAGS LAKE

Length: 4 miles round trip
Hiking time: 3 hours, day hike only
High point: 6,750 feet
Total elevation gain: 1,000 feet
Difficulty: moderate
Season: mid-June through late October
Water: available from streams and lake; purify first; best to bring your own
Maps: USGS 7.5' Manzanita Lake, park brochure
Permit: none required
Nearest campground: Manzanita Lake Campground
Information: Lassen Volcanic National Park

On this trail, you'll climb through a diverse and beautiful forest to Crags Lake, an obviously ephemeral body of water huddled under the

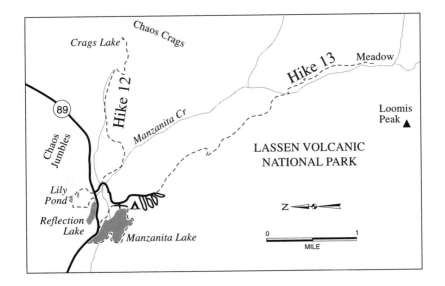

steep flanks of Chaos Crags, which periodically pummel the lake with small avalanches. You'll also have some good views thrown into the bargain.

To start the journey, reach the road to the Manzanita Lake Campground, which is on Highway 89's south side, 32.8 miles north of the junction of Highways 36 and 89, and 1.2 miles southeast of the junctions of Highways 44 and 89. Go 150 yards, then park in the lot on the left.

The path begins its ascent in an open forest featuring stately white fir and vanilla-scented Jeffrey pine. Look to the left at 0.1 mile for an impressive sugar pine (identifiable by its trademark foot-long cones). The forest soon deepens with the addition of red fir; note that several side trails will take you to the clear and tumbling waters of nearby Manzanita Creek.

Leave the proximity of the creek and descend to cross a small stream at 0.6 mile that's thickly shaded by white firs. The way runs level, then climbs. The tree cover thins at 1 mile as western white pines appear. Begin a steep climb past tobacco brush, greenleaf manzanita, pinemat manzanita, and bush chinquapin that doesn't relent until a relatively level stretch at 1.5 miles.

Climb some more, then reach at 1.9 miles the highlight of the hike: the ridge just above Crags Lake. Looming 1,700 feet above you, imposing and inhospitable Chaos Crags dominates the terrain. Nearly 2 miles in diameter, this impressive volcanic feature formed a little over a thousand years ago when thick, viscous lava welled up over 1,500 feet from a vent. You'll see very little in the way of green vegetation on the Crags, but there is a subtle display of purple-gray, rust, and orange-brown colors on the rock.

A glance down to the northwest reveals Chaos Jumbles, a massive avalanche that began at Chaos Crags around 300 years ago and extended nearly 3 miles to Manzanita Lake and beyond. Looking farther to the north, you'll see Hat Creek Valley and the high peaks of Thousand Lakes Wilderness; to the west, the peaks and hills of the Cascades eventually give way to the mighty Klamath Mountains.

Pick your way down to the shore of the lake by first leaving the main trail and heading for a flat area just to the north. Crags Lake can be gorgeous and inviting in years of high precipitation, but in most years it loses much of its volume and water clarity by late summer.

Nearby: Two nature trails offer a wealth of information. The Lily Pond Nature Trail starts across Highway 89 from the visitor center (Loomis Museum) 0.1 mile north of the turnoff to Manzanita Lake Campground. It travels a 1-mile loop, along which you can learn about many common plant species and area ecology and geology. The Indian Ways Nature Trail begins a mile northwest up Highway 89 from a roadside parking area. The 0.3 mile loop passes by several plants and dwellings used by local Indian tribes. The visitor center sells brochures for both trails; the brochure for the Lily Pond Nature Trail is also available at the trailhead.

13 MANZANITA CREEK

Length: 6.6 miles round trip
Hiking time: 4 hours or 2 days
High point: 6,850 feet
Total elevation gain: 1,050 feet
Difficulty: moderate
Season: mid-June through late October
Water: available from Manzanita Creek; purify first; best to bring your own
Maps: USGS 7.5' Manzanita Lake, USGS 7.5' Lassen Peak, park brochure
Permit: required for overnight trips; obtain from the Loomis Museum at the park's northwest entrance station, from the park's Mineral office, or from the Almanor Ranger District in Chester
Nearest campground: Manzanita Lake Campground
Information: Lassen Volcanic National Park

Map on page 45

On this hike, you'll walk through serene forests and lush meadows just 2 miles west of Chaos Crags and Lassen Peak, massive volcanoes that have been active within the last millennium. Manzanita Creek's clear, cold waters and numerous wildflowers also highlight the trip. If you wish to backpack, look for occasional level areas near the trail beyond the bridge across Manzanita Creek.

Travel Highway 89 for 32.8 miles north of the junction of Highways 36 and 89, or 1.2 miles southeast of the junctions of Highways 44 and 89. Turn south onto the road to Manzanita Lake Campground. Follow the road for 0.8 mile, then take Loop F around another 0.2 mile to the small parking area near site 31.

As you start on the sandy path, look above greenleaf manzanita and between Jeffrey pines and white firs at the stark visages of Chaos Crags and Lassen Peak. Continue on, then welcome the pleasing presence of red firs in the forest at 0.7 mile; staghorn lichens add fluorescent green to the trunks of both the red firs and white firs.

Climb steadily through the forest and reach an open, level area at 1.1 miles. Continue a very gentle ascent, then climb steeply as you note the presence of western white pines. Soon you'll have more views of Chaos Crags and Lassen Peak and will delight in the appearance of large quantities of lupine, coyote mint, penstemon, and gilia.

Reach the bridge across Manzanita Creek at 2 miles, a great spot to rest and watch the water flow beneath your feet and then disappear downhill amidst bordering flowers and mountain alder. When ready, continue past level areas for backpackers. You'll see Loomis Peak to the south at 2.4 miles. Featuring a serrated crest and multicolored steep cliffs that drop abruptly to near the west bank of Manzanita Creek, this impressive volcano will be the dominant topographical feature for the remainder of the hike.

Manzanita Lake and Lassen Peak

Note small meadows farther on near the creek, briefly travel through a dense red fir forest, then enter the first sizable meadow at 2.8 miles. Cross a small stream, then look north for views of Thousand Lakes Wilderness peaks.

The trail continues another 0.5 mile to a much larger meadow, verdant and moist, that bursts with a magical display of wildflowers in mid- and late summer. Faint paths traverse the meadow, but you may be content to sit on a log, enjoy a picnic, and gaze up at Loomis Peak and other surrounding ridges.

Nearby: A level 1.5-mile path circles large and beautiful Manzanita Lake, offering access to a wide variety of plant and animal life. Views can be breathtaking, especially the sight of Chaos Crags and Lassen Peak reflected in the waters from the north shore. Reach the trail just east of the park entrance station (park near the lake), from the picnic area on the east side of the lake, or from Manzanita Lake Campground.

14 CINDER CONE, SNAG LAKE, AND BUTTE LAKE LOOP

Length: 14 miles
Hiking time: 2 days
High point: 6,900 feet
Total elevation gain: 1,700 feet
Difficulty: moderate
Season: late June through October
Water: available only at Snag Lake, Grassy Creek, and Butte Lake; purify first
Maps: USGS 7.5' Prospect Peak, USGS 7.5' Mount Harkness, park brochure
Permit: required for overnight trips; obtain from the Loomis Museum at the park's northwest entrance station, from the park's Mineral office, or from the Almanor Ranger District in Chester
Nearest campground: Butte Creek Campground
Information: Lassen Volcanic National Park

This hike offers the best of Lassen Volcanic National Park: panoramic views from Cinder Cone's summit, mellow walking through forest and riparian areas, refreshing swimming in Snag and Butte lakes, and backcountry campsites that reveal the glory of the universe at night.

Drive Highway 44 east from its junction with Highway 89. After 11 miles, you'll see a sign for Butte Lake. Turn right and go 6 miles to Butte Lake Campground (which is closed indefinitely). Park in the lot by the lake's north shore.

Head over to the trail's beginning by the ranger station. After obtaining the informative interpretive nature and history brochure, begin walking the Nobles Emigrant Trail, as it passes the basalt flanks of the Fantastic Lava Beds. The trail was used in the 1850s and 1860s by pioneers.

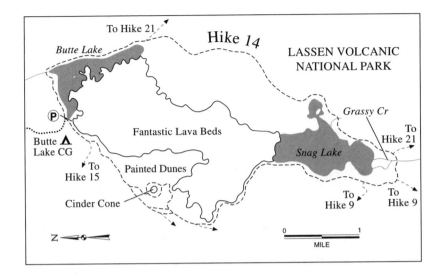

You'll soon reach a right-branching trail to the summit of Prospect Peak (hike 15). Go left and continue another mile to a trail fork at the base of Cinder Cone. (Backpackers will probably want to leave their packs at the base. Rejoin the main trail by continuing west on the Nobles Emigrant Trail, then curving south around Cinder Cone.)

The path heads straight up Cinder Cone, quickly gaining 750 feet of elevation and giving you a good workout. However, once atop the 6,900-foot rim, you'll be amply rewarded: Prospect Peak, Chaos Crags, Lassen Peak, Brokeoff Mountain, Reading Peak, and many other park landmarks vie for your long-distance attention. Much nearer to the east, Butte Lake and Snag Lake anchor the north and south ends of the Fantastic Lava Beds. This massive sheet of black basalt oozed from the base of Cinder Cone during a series of eruptions beginning with the volcano's formation about 425 years ago and ending about 265 years ago. Your eye will also be drawn to the orange and gray shades of the Painted Dunes just south of the cone, the result of hydrothermal action on volcanic ash.

When you're ready, head down the trail on the south side (or return for your pack). Go left at two trail forks in quick succession, then go left again 0.4 mile south at another trail fork. (A right turn takes you 2.2 miles to Rainbow Lake and the trails of hike 9.)

Arc southwest beside the Painted Dunes and the Fantastic Lava Beds and through a Jeffrey pine, lodgepole pine, and white fir forest. You'll soon reach Snag Lake, which formed about 300 years ago when basalt flows from Cinder Cone dammed Grassy Creek. You'll find several campsites around Snag Lake; take care not to camp too close to the shore.

The path continues 1.6 miles along the shore, then encounters two trail forks within 0.3 mile. Go left at both (a right at either connects you with hike 9). Travel 0.5 mile through a verdant paradise of spring-fed flowers, then go left again at another trail fork as you join part of hike 21.

Head northeast along Snag Lake's east shore and marvel at the stark beauty of Cinder Cone and the Fantastic Lava Beds across the

Butte Lake, Fantastic Lava Beds, Cinder Cone, and Prospect Peak from the east shore of Butte Lake

water. Walk through extensive aspen groves after leaving Snag Lake, then descend 3 miles through forest to a trail fork. A right would take you to Widow Lake via hike 21 and give you opportunities to explore the trails of the Caribou Wilderness (hikes 22 through 25).

To return to the trailhead, head north 1.6 miles just above Butte Lake's shore as you enjoy open vistas to the west and south. Climb steeply above the lake's outlet, then descend for the last 0.6 mile.

Nearby: For an easy saunter that's especially attractive on hot days, follow the trail from the parking area 0.4 mile north to Bathtub Lake for a swim in the relatively warm waters.

15 PROSPECT PEAK

Length: 6.4 miles round trip
Hiking time: 5 hours or 2 days
High point: 8,338 feet
Total elevation gain: 2,300 feet
Difficulty: moderate to strenuous
Season: early July through October
Water: none; bring at least 2 quarts per person
Maps: USGS 7.5' Prospect Peak, park brochure
Permit: required for overnight trips; obtain from the Loomis Museum at the park's northwest entrance station, from the park's Mineral office, or from the Almanor Ranger District in Chester
Nearest campground: Butte Creek Campground
Information: Lassen Volcanic National Park

The summit of Prospect Peak rewards you with outstanding vistas that encompass much of northern California. Adventurous souls in good shape may want to backpack this route and spend the night on

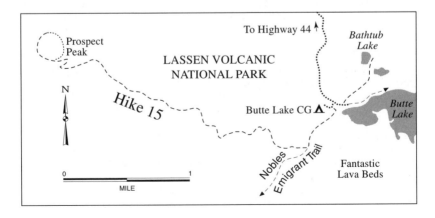

Cinder Cone and the Painted Dunes lie just south of Prospect Peak.

the summit. If you're one of these, bring plenty of water and check the weather report to be sure that there are no thunderstorms in the forecast (see the **Weather** section in the *Introduction* for information about safety and thunderstorms).

Drive Highway 44 east from its junction with Highway 89. After 11 miles, you'll see a sign for Butte Lake. Turn right and go 6 miles to Butte Lake Campground (which is closed indefinitely). Park in the lot by the lake's north shore.

Pick up the Cinder Cone interpretive brochure at the trailhead (located across from the ranger station); it explains the natural and human history of the path's first 0.4 mile along the Nobles Emigrant Trail. Walk beside the Fantastic Lava Beds, then take the right-hand trail at post 13 (hike 14 goes left to Cinder Cone and beyond).

Jeffrey, ponderosa, and Washoe pine needles litter the path as you begin the ascent of Prospect Peak. The Jeffrey pines soon take over the forest from their two close relatives, joined occasionally by white firs. As you go farther up the mountain, you'll pass through different vegetative zones dominated by different plants. Elevation, soil condition, and microclimate factors are the most important determinants of plant domination. The white firs soon succumb to this principle: Hardier red firs replace them. Significant ground-cover plants for much of the hike include pinemat manzanita, bush chinquapin, currant, buckwheat, native perennial grasses, and camphor-scented coyote mint. The orange flash and swooping flight of flickers add graceful animation to counterbalance the immobile trees.

Reach open country marked by stunted Jeffrey and western white pines 0.4 mile from the summit. Push up a set of switchbacks to reach the 8,338-foot summit proper, where you'll likely be greeted by noisy Clark's nutcrackers. Here a few mountain hemlocks and red firs join the Jeffrey and western white pines.

You now stand atop a cinder cone that's a geological cousin of the more famous "Cinder Cone" 2 miles southeast. This cinder cone literally capped the volcanic activity of Prospect Peak, a shield volcano formed from successive eruptions of liquid lava that spread from the mountain's summit and flanks to cover many square miles.

You can take a victory lap by following the trail around the cinder cone's rim or sit still and enjoy the bevy of vistas that stretch in all directions. Magee Peak and Burney Mountain rise to the northwest, with frosted Mount Shasta far beyond. The Medicine Lake Highlands lie east of Mount Shasta, with the Warner Mountains anchoring the northeastern vista. To the west, Raker Peak leads your eyes to imposing Chaos Crags and Lassen Peak, with the Sacramento Valley, Coast Range, and Klamath Mountains in the distance. Swinging south, you'll see Reading Peak, Mount Harkness, and the northern Sierra Nevada stretching to the hazy southern horizon. Near to the southeast are the park's Mount Hoffman and Red Cinder Cone, with the Caribou Wilderness just beyond. Range upon range of drier and drier mountains march east to Nevada. Cinder Cone, the Fantastic Lava Beds, the Painted Dunes, and Butte and Snag lakes lie just below.

Nearby: If you have more hiking energy, consider climbing Cinder Cone (hike 14). You also can take a leisurely walk along Butte Lake's north and east shorelines or head northeast from the trailhead 0.4 mile to swim in Bathtub Lake.

16 BOILING SPRINGS LAKE AND DEVIL'S KITCHEN

Length: 6.2 miles round trip
Hiking time: 4 hours or 2 days
High point: 6,000 feet
Total elevation gain: 800 feet
Difficulty: moderate
Season: early June through October
Water: bring your own
Map: USGS 7.5' Reading Peak
Permit: required for overnight trips, obtain from Loomis Museum at the park's northwest entrance station, from the park's Mineral office, or from the Almanor Ranger District in Chester
Nearest campground: Warner Valley Campground
Information: Lassen Volcanic National Park

The highlights of this hike are surface manifestations of the underground meeting of water and hot magma. The magma heats the water, which then dissolves minerals and gasses as it rises through cracks to Boiling Springs Lake and Devil's Kitchen. A nature trail describes various aspects of this volcanic activity that occurs at Boiling Springs Lake; you'll find the accompanying brochure at the trailhead. You'll also find far fewer people here at the isolated southern reaches of Lassen Park than at Bumpass Hell or Sulphur Works, which are home to similar volcanic phenomena. If you want to backpack, look for an occasional level area near the final mile to Devil's Kitchen, but remember that you must camp at least 0.25 mile from Devil's Kitchen.

Devil's Kitchen: a hotbed of geothermal turmoil (Photo by Marc J. Soares)

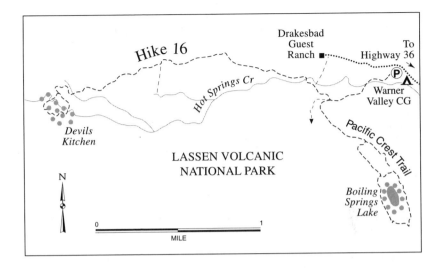

Reach Chester on Highway 36, go 100 feet east of the North Fork Feather River Bridge, then head north on Feather River Drive. Bear left after 0.7 mile, then, following signs for Drakesbad, go right after 6.2 miles onto Warner Valley Road. Continue another 10.4 miles to Warner Valley Campground, then reach the trailhead 0.3 mile farther. Note that the last two miles of dirt road are too rough for trailers.

Walk south and quickly reach Hot Springs Creek, a stream that drains through Devil's Kitchen, then courses east to merge with Kings Creek. Despite its name, Hot Springs Creek is quite cool.

Travel through a mixed forest of red and white fir, lodgepole and Jeffrey pine, and incense cedar. You'll reach an unusually large specimen of this latter species at post 9, where you'll also find two trail forks. Later, you'll take the first fork's right-hand trail to Devil's Kitchen; for now, go left at the two forks.

The obnoxious odor of hydrogen sulfide indicates the nearness of Boiling Springs Lake. Continue the ascent to the lake and its encircling trail, reached at 0.9 mile. Steam rises from the lake's bottom, heating the water to 125 degrees Fahrenheit. Look for dried-up mud pots, a steaming fumarole, and a good northwesterly view of Lassen Peak. For your safety, stay on the trail.

When you're ready for more hydrothermal theatrics, head back to the trail fork by the incense cedar and go left (west) for the 2-mile walk to Devil's Kitchen. Stay left when you encounter a path heading north to Drakesbad Guest Ranch, then cross Hot Springs Creek. Traverse a meadow, stay right at a trail fork, then climb gently through forest to the final destination, which features trails past fumaroles, mud pots, and steam vents (watch your step).

17 MOUNT HARKNESS

Length: 5.6 miles round trip
Hiking time: 4 hours or 2 days
High point: 8,045 feet
Total elevation gain: 1,350 feet
Difficulty: strenuous
Season: early July through mid-October
Water: none; bring at least 2 quarts per person for the day hike
Maps: USGS 7.5' Mount Harkness, park brochure
Permit: required for overnight trips; obtain from the Loomis Museum at the park's northwest entrance station, from the park's Mineral office, or from the Almanor Ranger District in Chester
Nearest campground: Juniper Lake Campground
Information: Lassen Volcanic National Park

Peak baggers will find Mount Harkness the easiest of Lassen Park's major summits to conquer. The view from the top is more than sufficient payment for the effort, but millions of wildflowers and a shoreline stroll along Juniper Lake make this hike a sure winner. Hard-core backpackers can find a few level spots among trees but must bring all water (camping is forbidden on or near the summit). Every hiker must take proper precautions regarding thunderstorms (see the **Weather** section in the *Introduction*).

Take Highway 36 to Chester, travel 100 feet east of the North Fork Feather River Bridge, then go north on Feather River Drive. Swing right after 0.7 mile. Enjoy the pavement for another 5.5 miles; then the road surface turns to rough dirt (too rough for trailers). Turn left into Juniper Lake Campground 12 miles from Highway 36 and park in the designated lot on the right. Walk to site 5 to find the trail.

Enjoy the initial level stretch before beginning a long, steep climb south between red firs and western white pines. The trail levels briefly at 1 mile as mountain hemlocks join the forest, then the ascent resumes westward to bring you into an open area with the hike's first views. Head back into a fairly level forest (take note, campers), then hit the open slopes for good. Continue past an extensive wealth of sky-blue lupines and sun-colored goldenbush.

Go left at a trail fork at 1.6 miles, then push uphill, spurred on by better and better views. Note the basalt flows as you continue onward; Mount Harkness, a shield volcano, formed from successive flows of liquid basalt. You soon leave the flows and switchback up the steep sides of the cinder cone that capped Harkness at the end of the mountain's major volcanic activity.

From the broad summit at 1.9 miles, you can circle the cinder cone's 100-foot-deep caldera and commiserate with the stunted trees that call these wind- and winter-swept heights home. But the panoramic vistas are the main attraction: To the west, Brokeoff Mountain, Lassen Peak,

A stunted Jeffrey pine is the forefront for a view of the Kings Creek drainage and Lassen Peak's entourage.

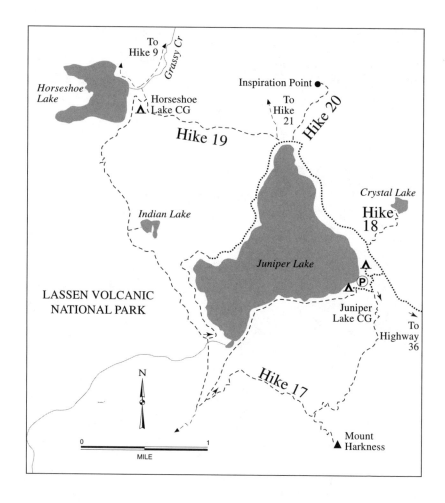

and Chaos Crags loom over the Kings Creek drainage and a host of lesser mountains; north beyond Juniper Lake are Hat Mountain, Magee Peak, and Burney Mountain just off Mount Shasta's east flank; Prospect and West Prospect peaks dominate due north, rising high above Cinder Cone; Red Cinder Cone, Red Cinder, North and South Caribou peaks and Caribou Wilderness forests lie to the east; Warner Valley, Lake Almanor, and the Sierra Nevada stretch to the south.

Drop back to the trail fork and go left for a steep descent through a forest that occasionally parts for good views to the west and north. Reach a few level areas suitable for a sleeping bag just before turning right at a trail fork that is 1.7 miles from the summit (a left leads 0.4 mile to hike 19). The final 1.8 miles take you to and then along the steep shore line of Juniper Lake and finally to the campground. Walk the road for the last 0.2 mile back to the parking area.

18   CRYSTAL LAKE

Length: 0.8 mile round trip
Hiking time: 1 hour, day hike only
High point: 7,250 feet
Total elevation gain: 450 feet
Difficulty: moderate
Season: late June through mid-October
Water: available at Crystal Lake; purify first
Maps: USGS 7.5' Mount Harkness, park brochure
Permit: none required
Nearest campground: Juniper Lake Campground
Information: Lassen Volcanic National Park

Map on page 58

This path rises at a rate of 1,125 feet per mile, which is mighty steep. However, since it's only 0.4 mile, you'll gladly accept the challenge to gain the good graces of Crystal Lake, one of the most precious jewels of Lassen Park. You can swim the inviting waters, picnic near the shores, explore nearby ridges, or just sit and absorb the beauty and magnificence of this special spot.

Drive Highway 36 to Chester, go 100 feet east of the North Fork Feather River Bridge, then head north on Feather River Drive. Bear right after 0.7 mile. Travel on pavement for another 5.5 miles; then the road surface turns to rough dirt (too rough for trailers). Continue 12.3 miles to the parking area on the right (0.3 mile past the turnoff to Juniper Lake Campground).

The trail to Crystal Lake allows an excellent panorama of Juniper Lake.

Start the brisk climb with the pleasant company of red fir, lodgepole pine, bush chinquapin, and pinemat manzanita as you travel near Crystal Lake's usually dry outlet creek. Continue up the rock-studded trail, noting the appearance of Jeffrey pine at 0.2 mile, along with a few greenleaf manzanita. Stop to gather energy and look west for impressive vistas, then push on with the certain knowledge that the views will be even better when you reach you destination. As you approach the last switchback before reaching Crystal Lake, look up to the right for a glimpse of a few western juniper trees, the namesake for Juniper Lake.

Let your pounding heart and bellowing lungs calm to normal rates as you take in the glacially formed lake and its near surroundings. The Crystal Cliffs and other ridges to the east rise 300 feet above the water's surface. To see these ridges reflected in the water, take a stroll along the 0.2-mile trail that circumnavigates the lake.

Climb the rocky knob on the south side of the outlet creek and park yourself near one of the western juniper trees. From here, you have an exquisite view: The broad expanse of Juniper Lake spreads out below, with the chain of prominent volcanoes from Brokeoff Peak to Lassen Peak and Chaos Crags jutting up farther to the west. Look south at the summit of Mount Harkness, then beyond to Lake Almanor and the broad spine of the northern Sierra Nevada.

19 HORSESHOE, INDIAN, AND JUNIPER LAKES LOOP

Length: 6.4 miles round trip
Hiking time: 4 hours or 2 days
High point: 7,100 feet
Total elevation gain: 950 feet
Difficulty: moderate
Season: late June through mid-October
Water: available only at lakes; purify first
Maps: USGS 7.5' Mount Harkness, park brochure
Permit: required for overnight trips; obtain from the Loomis Museum at the park's northwest entrance station, from the park's Mineral office, or from the Almanor Ranger District in Chester
Nearest campground: Juniper Lake Campground
Information: Lassen Volcanic National Park

Map on page 58

Large and beautiful lakes highlight this journey: You'll get a good taste of Juniper and Horseshoe lakes, plus smaller and more intimate Indian Lake. If you want a long backpacking journey, connect with hike 9 trails at Horseshoe Lake. For a longer and more strenuous day hike, climb Mount Harkness (hike 17).

Storm clouds gather over Horseshoe Lake.

Go to the town of Chester on Highway 36, then turn north onto Feather River Drive, which is 100 feet east of the North Fork Feather River Bridge. Swing right after 0.7 mile. The smooth pavement turns to rough dirt (too rough for trailers) after another 5.5 miles. The trailhead awaits 13.4 miles from Highway 36 at Juniper Lake's north shore.

Walk west past the small cabins to the sign at the trailhead. The path begins a moderate 0.6-mile ascent through an open forest of lodgepole pines, western white pines, and red firs. Look behind for eastward glimpses of Juniper Lake and Crystal Cliffs.

The path levels, then descends, allowing westward views of Brokeoff Mountain, Lassen Peak, and Chaos Crags. At 1.4 miles, you'll reach Horseshoe Lake, named for its two westward-extending arms. Like Juniper Lake, Horseshoe Lake owes its existence to past glacial action that deepened and widened existing depressions in the volcanic landscape. Enjoy views of Lassen Peak and Mount Harkness and consider hiking west along the north shore or north along the lush environs of Grassy Creek (see hike 9).

To continue, take the path near the campground and along the east and south shores, then climb relatively steeply. Shortly before the climb ends, the forest once again parts, this time for the best views of the entire hike: Lassen Peak and Chaos Crags in full glory to the west, forested valley and ridge to the northwest, and Prospect Peak and West Prospect Peak to the north.

The trail soon crests, then runs fairly level to the side trail to Indian Lake at 2.8 miles. Here you'll find adequate swimming spots and a few level areas for camping, if you're so inclined.

Descend gently past a few ponds and enjoy views of Mount Harkness straight ahead, then reach a trail fork at 4.1 miles. A right connects you after 0.4 mile with hike 17 (Mount Harkness) and a 1.8-mile walk to Juniper Lake Campground.

To complete the loop, go left and undulate along Juniper Lake's west shore, where you'll enjoy views of Lassen Park's largest lake. You also can look east to Crystal Cliffs and the ledge holding Crystal Lake; both harbor the juniper trees for which Juniper Lake was named. It's 2.3 miles back to the trailhead, the last part on a road.

20 INSPIRATION POINT

Length: 1.4 miles round trip
Hiking time: 2 hours, day hike only
High point: 7,202 feet
Total elevation gain: 400 feet
Difficulty: moderate
Season: late June through mid-October
Water: none; bring your own
Maps: USGS 7.5' Mount Harkness, park brochure
Permit: none required
Nearest campground: Juniper Lake Campground
Information: Lassen Volcanic National Park

Map on page 58

The climb to Inspiration Point certainly gets the heart pumping. But considering that the trail travels a modest 0.7 mile and ends at a relatively low final elevation, Inspiration Point offers surprisingly good views of Lassen Park lakes and peaks.

On Highway 36 in Chester, go 100 feet east of the North Fork Feather River Bridge and turn north on Feather River Drive. Bear right after 0.7 mile. The pavement lasts another 5.5 miles; the road runs rough the rest of the way (too rough for trailers). Reach trailhead parking near Juniper Lake's north shore 13.4 miles from Highway 36. The hike begins just east of the parking area.

The path starts nearly level as it travels through a forest of lodgepole pine, western white pine, and red fir that shades an understory of pinemat manzanita and grasses. However, the way soon steepens as the forest opens. Look 100 feet to the left at 0.3 mile for a large, weather-battered Jeffrey pine; then, just before the top, see greenleaf manzanita and a small thicket of bush chinquapin.

Crest the top of Inspiration Point at 0.6 mile. From here, the trail goes another 200 yards along a ridge populated by white firs and the previously encountered tree species. When you look beyond the immediate surroundings to the encircling mountainous tableau, you'll agree that Inspiration Point deserves its name. To the south, Crystal Cliffs guards the broad expanse of Juniper Lake, with Mount Harkness just beyond and the northern Sierra Nevada stretching off into a gauze of haze. Swinging westward, Saddle Mountain, Pilot Mountain, and Mount Conard lead to the dominating range anchored by Brokeoff Peak and Chaos Crags and centered by Lassen Peak. To the northwest rise Magee Peak and distant Mount Shasta, while more due north are Prospect Peak and West Prospect Peak, Cinder Cone, Fantastic Lava Beds, Snag Lake, and Mount Hoffman. To the east, forested slopes stretch into the Caribou Wilderness.

Mount Hoffman rises beyond the red firs and western white pines of Inspiration Point.

21   SNAG, WIDOW, AND JAKEY LAKES

Length: 17 miles round trip
Hiking time: 2 or 3 days
High point: 7,650 feet
Total elevation gain: 2,300 feet
Difficulty: moderate
Season: late June through mid-October
Water: sporadically available at lakes; purify first; always have 1 quart per person on hand
Maps: USGS 7.5' Mount Harkness, USGS 7.5' Prospect Peak, park brochure
Permit: required for overnight trips; obtain from the Loomis Museum at the park's northwest entrance station, from the park's Mineral office, or from the Almanor Ranger District in Chester
Nearest campground: Juniper Lake Campground
Information: Lassen Volcanic National Park

Lakes large and small and a variety of volcanic landscapes await backpackers who travel in this seldom-visited eastern realm of Lassen

Jakey Lake is one of the many bodies of water encountered on hike 21.

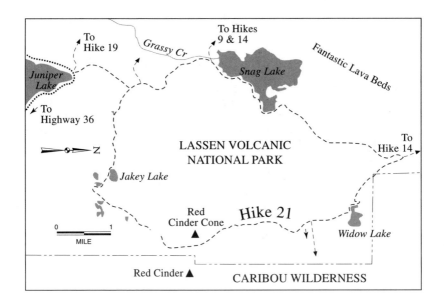

Park. For more extensive treks, you have the option of connecting with hikes 9, 14, and 22 through 25.

Reach Chester, go 100 feet east of the North Fork Feather River Bridge on Highway 36, and turn north on Feather River Drive. Go right after 0.7 mile. Drive on pavement the next 5.5 miles; then the road turns to rough dirt (too rough for trailers). The trailhead is at Juniper Lake's north shore, 13.4 miles from Highway 36. Park in the large lot on the right.

Head west past three small cabins and a park rules sign, then turn right. Climb through a forest of red fir, western white pine, and lodgepole pine, species that will dominate the forest for the entire hike, with the occasional addition of white fir and Jeffrey pine.

Reach a saddle at 0.4 mile, then drop steeply to a trail fork at 1.3 miles. The trail to the right is your return route. Go left, cross a stream, then go right at another trail fork 0.3 mile farther (a left takes you a mile to Grassy Creek and hike 9).

Descend past several small, flower-strewn meadows to another trail fork at 2.9 miles. A left would quickly bring you to hike 9 paths, but go right, sharing the east shore of Snag Lake and its many campsites and swimming spots with hike 14.

As you continue, look north for views of the Fantastic Lava Beds, Cinder Cone, and Prospect Peak. After leaving Snag Lake, walk through an extensive aspen grove, climb briefly, then descend to a trail fork at 6.9 miles.

Consider a visit to Butte Lake 0.2 mile down the left. Then head right for the 1.3-mile climb along Widow Lake's outlet creek (dry from midsummer on) to Widow Lake. This secluded lake invites you to spend the night at any of the numerous campsites spread around its shores.

A trail running 2.6 miles east to Triangle Lake in the Caribou Wilderness and hikes 22 through 25 goes left 0.9 mile south of Widow Lake. Continue to climb towards Red Cinder and Red Cinder Cone, noting the hardy mountain hemlocks that appear as you approach a saddle between the two at 11.5 miles. Experienced cross-country hikers armed with topographical maps can tackle the summit of Red Cinder Cone to the west and thus gain good views of Lassen Park and Caribou Wilderness terrain.

From the saddle, the hike's highest elevation, descend gently through forest. Soon small trailside lakes offer visual relief; some are deep enough for swimming and have level areas for camping. The largest, Jakey Lake at 14.2 miles, features camping near the west shore and swimming along the north shore.

The route then travels near Jakey Lake's outlet stream and hosts coyote mint, yarrow, and lupines on the forest floor. Several small meadows and a large pond line this final 1.5 miles to the previously encountered trail fork just north of Juniper Lake. From here, it's 1.3 miles to the trailhead.

NEAR LASSEN VOLCANIC NATIONAL PARK

Early autumn storm clouds and Lake Eiler

22 BEAUTY, POSEY, AND LONG LAKES LOOP

Length: 7.1 miles round trip
Hiking time: 5 hours or 2 days
High point: 7,000 feet
Total elevation gain: 700 feet
Difficulty: easy
Season: mid-June through late October; many mosquitoes through late July
Water: available from numerous lakes; purify first
Map: USGS 7.5' Red Cinder
Permit: none required
Nearest campgrounds: Silver Bowl Campground, Rocky Knoll Campground
Information: Almanor Ranger District, Lassen National Forest

This easy walk in the southern reaches of the Caribou Wilderness visits over a dozen lakes and takes you through virgin forests bursting with flowers and birds. The gentle terrain makes hiking easy, so this is a good trip for children and first-time backpackers. Surprisingly, you'll share this beautiful country with few others. If you desire a longer journey, it's easy to connect with hikes 21 and 23 through 25.

Reach Chester, then head east on Highway 36. From the eastern edge of Lake Almanor's north arm, continue 3.5 miles, then go left onto Forest Road 10 where Road A13 goes right. Stay on this paved road for 10.2 miles. When the pavement ends, go left onto a dirt road for the final 1.6 miles to the Hay Meadow trailhead. (Continuing north 10.7 miles on M10 brings you to the trailhead for hikes 23 and 24.)

Verdant Hay Meadow, punctuated by willows and decorated by

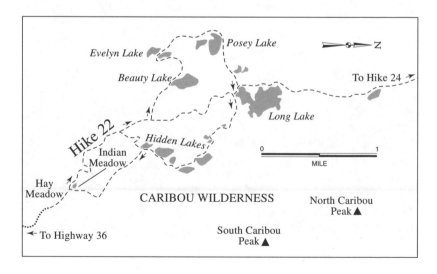

flowers, presages the natural beauty of the entire hike. You'll soon reach the registration area and sign in; then go left at a trail fork at 0.3 mile (you'll return via the right-hand trail). Border Indian Meadow and cross the outlet of its small pond.

The trail leads uphill through a forest of red and white firs and western white and lodgepole pines, the primary tree species encountered on the hike. Go left at a trail fork at 1.2 miles and left once more at another trail fork at 1.5 miles. (The 1.2-mile trail to the right runs directly to Long Lake).

Ramble leisurely a half mile up the moderate gradient to the shores of Beauty Lake. Like most of the lakes in Caribou Wilderness, this lake

Red firs frame a view of Beauty Lake.

is surrounded by forest. The side trail along the west side goes to several established campsites and takes you to the northern edge, which hosts good swimming and an aspen grove.

A smaller, deeper, and more intimate lake awaits another 0.3 mile farther. A rock cliff abuts its north shore near a good campsite. From here, continue to Evelyn Lake at 2.4 miles, where a volcanic ridge guards the lake's western shore. A side trail to the right leads to a campsite.

Continue on the main (though fainter) path and ascend moderately through the forest to reach Posey Lake at 3.1 miles. This lake features numerous campsites and good swimming.

Descend to a trail fork at 3.7 miles and go briefly left to visit Long Lake. From the western shore, the shallow waters reflect the enticing images of North and South Caribou peaks, which together anchor the Caribou Wilderness' eastern realm. Continuing north 3 miles on this trail brings you to North and South Divide Lakes and the opportunity to explore the northern parts of the wilderness (hikes 23 through 25) or head into Lassen Park (hike 21). If you need a campsite, look on the lake's south side.

To complete the loop, head back to the trail fork and go left. Go left at another fork shortly thereafter (a right is the just-mentioned short-cut) and enjoy mostly downhill walking.

A pond on the right at 4.2 miles signals the beginning of the Hidden Lakes. True to their name, several of the lakes lie unseen behind ridges. Follow the faint side paths and explore on your own. Campsites are relatively abundant.

The last hidden lake rests on the right at 5.4 miles just before a trail fork (go left). Drop down through the forest and reach Indian Meadow at 6.5 miles. Skirt the eastern edge, then go left at a previously encountered trail fork for the last 0.3 mile to the trailhead.

23 EMERALD, RIM, AND CYPRESS LAKES

Length: 7.4 miles round trip
Hiking time: 5 hours or 2 days
High point: 7,100 feet
Total elevation gain: 700 feet
Difficulty: easy to moderate
Season: mid-June through late October; many mosquitoes through late July
Water: available from lakes; purify first
Maps: USGS 7.5' Harvey Mountain, USGS 7.5' Red Cinder
Permit: none required
Nearest campgrounds: Silver Bowl Campground, Rocky Knoll Campground
Information: Almanor Ranger District, Lassen National Forest

This trip features the best scenery of all the trails in Caribou Wilderness: You'll visit three of the area's most beautiful lakes and have

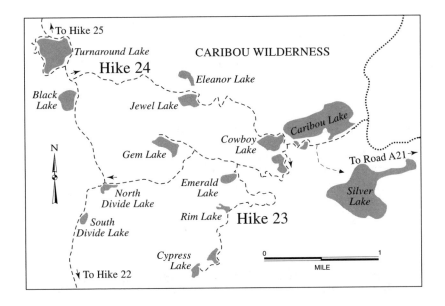

expansive vistas of the surrounding terrain. All or part of hikes 21, 22, 24, and 25 can be combined with this one to make a major expedition.

Drive Road A21 4.5 miles southwest from its junction with Highway 44 or 14 miles north of Westwood. Go west on Silver Lake Road (also called Mooney Road) for 6 miles, then go right on Road M10 (a left heads 12 miles to the hike 22 trailhead). Follow M10 and trailhead signs for the final mile.

To find the trailhead, go 50 yards uphill to a signboard for the wilderness (where you sign in). Head west above Caribou Lake through a red fir, lodgepole pine, and Jeffrey pine forest. Stay right at 0.4 mile when a trail to Silver Lake heads left near the wilderness boundary.

Go left at 0.7 mile and walk around a shallow figure-eight lake. Begin a moderate ascent at 1 mile that brings you to a trail fork at 1.7 miles.

Hike 24 goes right, but you go left to reach at 1.8 miles a coveted view of Emerald Lake. From the large campsite on a north-side cliff, you can gaze at the green glints of this aqueous jewel, which invites you to immerse yourself in its cleansing waters.

The path heads east through open country to eventually swing around and head west. You'll approach an escarpment at 2.7 miles. Walk the 50 feet from the trail to its edge for prime views of the tops of western white pines (cones drooping) and red firs (cones erect) and mountains and lakes to the north, east, and west. This is also a good spot to sit quietly and observe wildlife.

Rim Lake awaits another 0.2 mile up the trail. The ridge near its north shore gives the best panorama available from a Caribou Wilderness trail. Swimmers will find deep water near the southwest shore. There are no actual campsites, but you'll find plenty of level ground.

Walk southwest from Rim Lake to an unnamed, shallow lake at 3.5 miles that has a few campsites and an impressive westward view of a steep cliff. Deeper Cypress Lake lies another 0.2 mile farther and also has campsites.

North Caribou Peak rises to an elevation of 7,793 feet about a half mile southeast of Cypress Lake. Intermittent trails and occasional rock piles can guide you to the summit, where vistas of prominent Lassen Park landmarks and the northern Sierra Nevada await. Attempt this side trip only if you're experienced at cross-country hiking (especially rock scrambling) and have a compass and topographical map (and know how to use them).

Jeffrey pine branch and Emerald Lake

24 GEM, BLACK, AND COWBOY LAKES LOOP

Length: 7.5 miles round trip
Hiking time: 5 hours or 2 days
High point: 7,000 feet
Total elevation gain: 500 feet
Difficulty: easy
Season: mid-June through late October; many mosquitoes through late July
Water: available from lakes; purify first
Maps: USGS 7.5' Bogard Buttes, USGS 7.5' Red Cinder
Permit: none required
Nearest campgrounds: Silver Bowl Campground, Rocky Knoll Campground
Information: Almanor Ranger District, Lassen National Forest

Map on page 71

This easy loop trail takes you past numerous lakes and ponds in the heart of the Caribou Wilderness. The path stays primarily in the forest, so if you want views of Lassen Peak and other nearby mountains, visit the more open terrain of hike 23 as a side trip. You also can make an extended excursion by connecting with hikes 21, 22, and 25.

Take Road A21 for 14 miles north of Westwood or 4.5 miles southwest from its junction with Highway 44 and then head west on Silver Lake Road (also called Mooney Road). After 6 miles, go right on Road M10 (a left here takes you 12 miles to the hike 22 trailhead). Follow M10 and trailhead signs for the final mile.

Head uphill 50 yards to find a signboard/trail register (sign in) that displays the Caribou Wilderness brochure. Begin above Caribou Lake's dam and walk west above the lake's south shore for 0.3 mile through a forest of lodgepole pine, red fir, and Jeffrey pine. These trees, along with some western white pines, accompany you for the rest of the journey.

Stay right at 0.4 mile when a trail from Silver Lake comes in on the left just before the wilderness boundary. Pass between twin lily-pad ponds, then reach another trail fork at 0.7 mile (you'll return via the right-hand fork). Go left and circle around a shallow hourglass-shaped lake.

A moderate climb commences at 1 mile and doesn't let up until you reach a trail junction at 1.7 miles. Hike 23 covers the left-hand trail. Even if you don't have time for all of hike 23, do go the 150 yards to Emerald Lake, one of the Caribou Wilderness' most beautiful water bodies (and it has a great campsite).

The main trail gently rises as it heads west to another trail fork at 2.1 miles. A 300-yard side trip right to the deep waters of Gem Lake is especially tempting if you want to swim, but the lake has no good campsites.

Continue another mile to shallow North Divide Lake and another trail fork. A left would take you 0.3 mile to South Divide Lake (which offers better camping than its sibling) and then another 2 miles to Long Lake and the trails of hike 22.

Looking west from the east shore of Black Lake

Head right and travel north 0.8 mile to the southeast shore of grass-lined Black Lake. Here you'll find camping on the north and south sides.

Reach a trail fork just north of Black Lake. Go right (a left connects with hike 25 after 0.2 mile), climb eastward, descend, then walk fairly level to Jewel Lake, 1.5 miles from the trail fork. Jewel Lake features deep water and campsites near the north shore. Eleanor Lake lies 150 yards north on the opposite side of the trail.

From Jewel Lake, descend 1.1 miles to shallow Cowboy Lake, then quickly come to a previously encountered trail fork. Go left for the final 0.7 mile back to the trailhead.

25 TRIANGLE AND TURNAROUND LAKES

Length: 7.8 miles round trip
Hiking time: 5 hours or 2 days
High point: 7,100 feet
Total elevation gain: 600 feet
Difficulty: easy
Season: mid-June through late October; many mosquitoes through late July
Water: available from lakes; purify first
Map: USGS 7.5' Bogard Buttes
Permit: none required
Nearest campgrounds: Silver Bowl Campground, Rocky Knoll Campground
Information: Almanor Ranger District, Lassen National Forest

Easy walking and beautiful lakes highlight this hike into the northern part of the Caribou Wilderness. Backpackers can take a trail west into Lassen Park and join hike 21, or they can wander farther into the Caribou Wilderness with hikes 22 through 24.

To find the trailhead, take Forest Road 10 from Highway 44's west side. This point is 18 miles southeast of the junctions of Highways 89 and 44 near Old Station, 34 miles northwest of Susanville, 4.7 miles northwest of the junction with Road A21, and 150 yards south of a highway rest stop. Follow Road 10 west for 5.8 miles, then go right onto Road 32N09 for the last 2.8 miles. (Staying left on M10 will take you 5 miles to the trailhead for hikes 23 and 24.)

The trail begins by Cone Lake, which usually dries up by midsummer. Sign in at the trail register, then walk past a grove of aspen. The path passes through an open Jeffrey pine forest as it climbs ever so gently past an understory of pinemat manzanita, squaw carpet, coyote mint, rabbitbrush goldenweed, and lupines and other flowers.

Reach a double-trunked Jeffrey pine at 0.2 mile, then notice how the tree diversity increases to include red fir and lodgepole pine. By the time you reach a pond at 1.7 miles, the Jeffreys have mostly disappeared, leaving the lodgepoles to dominate the rest of the hike.

Large and luscious Triangle Lake lies just beyond the pond. Swim the waters from the northern shores and enjoy views of Red Cinder to the southwest and Black Butte to the north from the east shore. A 1.2-mile circumnavigating trail heads west from the north shore, initially passing a good campsite, and then leads to others equally impressive on the west shore before rejoining the main trail at Twin Lakes. (The trail to Lassen Park and hike 21 begins near the lake's northwest corner. It heads west for 2.6 miles, intersecting hike 21 0.9 mile south of Widow Lake.)

Farther south along the main trail, the Twin Lakes appear at 2.5 miles. Though not as spectacular as the lake you left or Turnaround Lake to come, the Twin Lakes have level places to camp and offer solitude if the more popular lakes are too crowded.

Lodgepole-pine-bordered Turnaround Lake appears at 3.2 miles. Flanked by 200-foot-high ridges on the east and west, it boasts deep

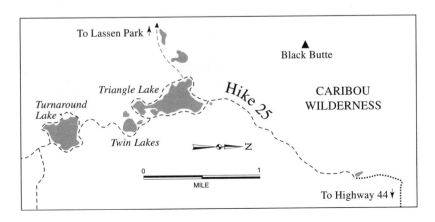

Triangle Lake and Red Cinder

waters, a trail around its circumference, and campsites near the north and east sides. Following the path around the lake's east edge brings you to a trail fork and the paths of hike 24 at 3.9 miles.

26

BIZZ JOHNSON TRAIL: DEVIL'S CORRAL TO SUSANVILLE

Length: 13.4 miles round trip
Hiking time: 7 hours or 2 days
High point: 4,660 feet
Total elevation gain: 450 feet
Difficulty: easy
Season: early May to early November; prettiest in May
Water: available from the Susan River; purify first
Maps: USGS 7.5' Roop Mountain, USGS 7.5' Susanville
Permit: none required
Nearest campground: Merrill Campground
Information: Eagle Lake Resource Area, Bureau of Land Management

The Susan River emerges from mountain lakes near the Caribou Wilderness and flows southeast to empty into Honey Lake. This hike takes you through a scenic section of the river canyon that shelters a large variety of plant and animal life and offers a large dose of human history. Note that you can backpack the trail, but its heavy use by mountain bikers and other hikers means that you'd have little privacy. If you do camp, find a site that's at least a mile downstream of the trailhead and a mile upstream of Susanville's outskirts (look for signs). The walk is described here as beginning at Devil's Corral, but you also can begin it from Susanville or arrange for a car shuttle.

Travel Highway 36 to the signed Devil's Corral trail-access point, which is on the south side of the highway and just east of the bridge across the Susan River, 14 miles east of Westwood and 7 miles west of Susanville. Follow the paved road 0.2 mile to the parking area. (To reach the Susanville end of the hike, take Highway 36 to Susanville and head south on Weatherlow Street, which eventually becomes Richmond Road. Follow Richmond Road to the trail-access point at

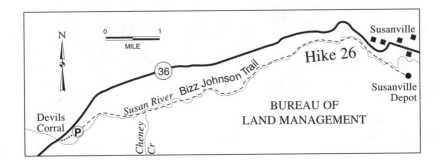

the historic Susanville railroad depot, which is about 0.5 mile from Highway 36.)

As you begin the hike, note that the trail is wide and flat with a very gentle grade—it once held the tracks of the Fernley and Lassen Railroad. In operation from 1914 to 1956, the railroad serviced the local timber industry. As you walk the trail, note the mixture of plant habitats: Drier areas hold western juniper, sagebrush, and antelopebrush; moister areas feature ponderosa pine, Douglas fir, and white fir; and the river's waters allow streamside willows and black cottonwoods to flourish.

You'll soon catch the first view of the Susan River, which will be your constant companion for the remainder of the hike. At 1.3 miles, cross the river on the first of several wooden bridges, then see Cheney Creek tumble in from the south. (Campers: This is the only spot where fires are allowed.) Inspect the canyon walls; they're composed of basalt that began as fluid lava that flowed for miles before cooling. Look for the bands separating successive flows and for the columnar jointing that cracked the basalt as it cooled.

Reach a tunnel at 1.7 miles. Its cool and dusky recesses offer welcome respite from the heat and light outside, and its damp and musty

Hikers on the Bizz Johnson Trail cross the Susan River on a bridge.

smell will remind you of a wine cellar. (A good swimming hole is just upstream from the tunnel's east end.) Pass through a second tunnel at 2 miles, then take a rest on a log bench situated under the shade of a ponderosa pine at 2.8 miles.

The way continues east past the Susan River's tumbling waters. The stream slows enough to allow swimming under a bridge at 5.3 miles and farther downstream near sandbars accessed by side trails. Susanville and civilization appear at 6 miles, and at 6.7 miles, you'll reach the Susanville railroad depot, which has a visitor center, outside interpretive displays, and an information kiosk.

If you wish to explore more of the Bizz Johnson Trail's 29-mile length, consider hiking upstream 6 miles from Devil's Corral to Goumaz. For information on this section and on the rest of the trail, contact the Eagle Lake Ranger District (477–050 Eagle Lake Road, Susanville, CA 96130, tel.: 916-257-4188).

27 DEER CREEK

Length: 4.6 miles round trip
Hiking time: 3 hours
High point: 3,250 feet
Total elevation gain: 650 feet
Difficulty: moderate
Season: year-round; occasional winter snow
Water: available from Deer Creek and tributaries; purify first
Map: USGS 7.5' Onion Butte
Permit: none required
Nearest campground: Potato Patch Campground
Information: Almanor Ranger District, Lassen National Forest

The crashing cacophony of Deer Creek provides constant company as you travel downstream past several small waterfalls and one large cataract. The trail leaves directly from Highway 32, so you can wander near the creek and high up the canyon walls anytime there is no snow. You'll also find at least a dozen level areas to camp along the route, making this hike a good spring warm-up for high-country backpacking or a good introduction to backpacking for beginners. Trout anglers will find several side trails to the creek banks.

From Chico, take Highway 32 off Highway 99 and drive 40 miles north to the first bridge across Deer Creek (it's terra-cotta-colored) and park in the area on the right, 100 feet beyond. The parking area is also 1.6 miles southwest of Potato Patch Campground. Note that Highway 32 has many curves and is not recommended for motor homes and vehicles with trailers.

Cross the road to the northeast side of the bridge and find the route near the Deer Creek Trail sign. Walk in the shade of Douglas fir (the vicinity's dominant tree), ponderosa pine, incense cedar, and canyon

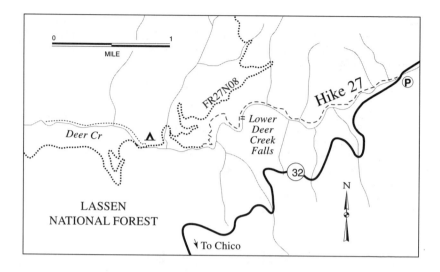

live oak to the first of several small streams that feed Deer Creek. Shortly beyond, a large outcropping of volcanic rock just above Deer Creek provides an excellent vantage point for watching the swift water course between white alders southwest toward the Sacramento River.

Look for a small cave on the right at 0.4 mile, then note the first appearance of California nutmeg, an uncommon tree species easily identified by its sharp, dark-green needles. The path passes several level spots suitable for camping, then travels above a series of waterfalls at 1.1 miles. After climbing partway up the hillside, you'll traverse a level stretch under a canopy of tall canyon live oaks.

Lower Deer Creek Falls, the main attraction, awaits at 1.6 miles: Take the two-pronged side trail to the downstream edge of a massive, churning waterfall that drops 15 feet to shoot a steady spray of fine mist on your face. When you can break the hypnosis of the falls, look around at the canyon walls stretching 1,000 feet above.

When you eventually tear yourself away, continue on the main track past several more camping areas, then up through fragrant groves of California laurel to more views of the canyon. You'll eventually make a steep descent to the end of the trail (and several campsites) near Deer Creek at 2.3 miles.

If you haven't yet satisfied your wanderlust, follow the dirt road a half mile in the downstream direction to Forest Road 27NO8. Turn left and walk another 0.3 mile to a primitive campground on the right-hand side that's just 100 feet north of a bridge across Deer Creek. Head through the campground to an old, unmaintained trail that continues over logs and across streams for another mile or so before totally petering out. If you wish to arrange a car shuttle, have someone take Forest Road 27NO8 from Highway 32 (3.6 miles southwest of the parking area, 36.4 miles north of Highway 99; it is signed for Deer Creek) and drive 6 miles to the bridge.

Deer Creek and the Deer Creek Canyon just upstream of Lower Deer Creek Falls

28 LOWER MILL CREEK: NORTH SIDE

Length: 9.4 miles round trip
Hiking time: 6 hours or 2 days
High point: 2,100 feet
Total elevation gain: 500 feet
Difficulty: easy to moderate
Season: late April through November; very hot in summer
Water: available from Mill Creek and smaller streams; purify first
Maps: USGS 7.5' Barkley Mountain, USGS 7.5' Panther Spring
Permit: none required
Nearest campground: Black Rock Campground
Information: Almanor Ranger District, Lassen National Forest

This hike in the Ishi Wilderness combines all the area's attractions: a steep lava-rock canyon, a bounty of wildflowers, and the cool waters of Mill Creek, a year-round stream that's accessible via several side trails. Backpackers will find a few level spots to pitch a tent or roll out a sleeping bag. This hike also takes you through land once inhabited by the Yahi Indians. A Yahi named Ishi and a few companions hid from European-American persecution in the Mill Creek and Deer Creek canyons beginning in 1870. Ishi, the last surviving member of his tribe, walked to Oroville in 1911. He spent his remaining few years teaching anthropologists about his culture. For more exploration of the Mill Creek canyon, take the path upstream past Black Rock (see hike 30) or do hike 29 (Lower Mill Creek: South Side).

The trailhead waits at Black Rock Campground. Drive Highway 36 to Paynes Creek. Head south on Paynes Creek Road for 0.3 mile, turn right onto Plum Creek Road, go 8 miles, then turn right onto Ponderosa Way (Road 28N29). Travel Ponderosa Way's dirt and rock surface for 20 miles (which can be difficult after a rain), always following signs for Black Rock and Mill Creek. Note that you'll have to drive through

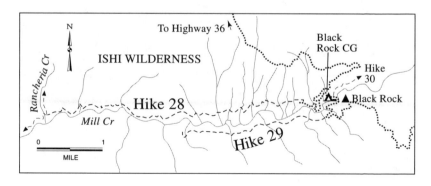

A buckeye tree in bloom and the Mill Creek Canyon west of Black Rock

the North Fork of Antelope Creek on top of a cement culvert, which can be difficult when water flow is high.

Find the signed trail at the west end of Black Rock Campground. It climbs briefly to join a dirt road; follow the road 0.3 mile to a gate for a private ranch, then go right and pass through another gate. For the next 0.4 mile, you traverse a series of wet, spring-fed meadows.

Beyond the ranch, the true wilderness begins as the trail undulates along the hillside. Blue, black, and interior live oaks predominate on the open, grassy slopes, with canyon live oaks and California laurel inhabiting the cooler and moister ravines. Gray pine is the most common large tree, but occasionally a stand of ponderosa pines stakes a claim to a flat area near Mill Creek. Most of the rock is basaltic and thus of volcanic origin, but a sharp eye will spy a few areas of sedimentary rock. You'll notice evidence on the south side of the canyon of large fires that burned through here in 1990 and 1994.

Enter another meadow at 3 miles. Continue to a crossing of Avery Creek, then reach the Rancheria Trail at 4.7 miles. If you want to hike farther, head up this faint path, or continue a bit farther downstream along the Mill Creek Trail.

29 LOWER MILL CREEK: SOUTH SIDE

Length: 5.2 miles round trip
Hiking time: 3 hours or 2 days
High point: 2,200 feet
Total elevation gain: 400 feet
Difficulty: easy to moderate
Season: mid-April through November; very hot in summer
Water: available from Mill Creek and smaller streams; purify first
Map: USGS 7.5' Barkley Mountain
Permit: none required
Nearest campground: Black Rock Campground
Information: Almanor Ranger District, Lassen National Forest

Map on page 82

This walk along the slope just south of Mill Creek gives you long-range vistas of steep-sided Mill Creek Canyon, yet it also takes you past several intimate and shady streams. The open hillsides offer a special treat: effusive eruptions of wildflowers in late spring. There are no obvious campsites, but you'll find many level spots if backpacking suits you. Poison oak borders several stretches of trail, so wear long pants and watch with a wary eye for leaves of three.

Drive Highway 36 to Paynes Creek, then turn south onto Paynes Creek Road. After 0.3 mile, turn right onto Plum Creek Road. Go 8 miles, then turn right onto Ponderosa Way (Road 28N29), the dirt road you'll travel 20 miles to Black Rock Campground. (Ponderosa Way can be difficult to navigate after a rain.) Note that you'll have to drive through the North Fork of Antelope Creek on top of a cement culvert, which can be tricky when water flow is high. Follow signs for Mill Creek and the campground at all intersections. Pass Black Rock Campground and climb 0.4 mile beyond Mill Creek to the signed trailhead on the west side of the road just below Black Rock.

The trail begins under the spread branches of a large blue oak, then heads downhill past more of the same species, plus black oak and interior live oak. You'll also see several buckeye trees, noted by their groups of five or seven palmate leaves and large white flower spikes. Canyon live oaks form a dense crown over a small stream at 0.1 mile and then you'll glimpse Mill Creek rushing below. Though Mill Creek plays a constant serenade, you won't see it again until the end of the hike.

Soon the way reaches a spring bordered by white alders adorned with gnarled vines of wild grape. Just beyond, you'll observe black scars on ponderosa pines and other trees, the reminders of recent fire in the Ishi Wilderness. At 0.5 mile, look north beyond Mill Creek: The lava cap rim tops more volcanic outcrops, with lush meadows below.

Pass two more small streams (the second bordered by spice-scented California laurel), then climb a hill for a good view east of Black Rock and the upper Mill Creek canyon. Follow rock ducks across a grassy slope filled with the gorgeous yellow petals of tarweed in spring, then descend to a creek at 1.5 miles. Upon the ascent out, look to the right for a sharp-needled California nutmeg tree.

An upstream view of Mill Creek from the vantage point at the end of hike 29

Undulate along the hillside, cross another stream at 2.0 miles (look for incense cedar and bigleaf maple), then enjoy good westward views of the chaparral slopes of the lower canyon tailing off toward the Sacramento Valley. Drop down to the last creek crossing at 2.6 miles, noting the layers of lava rock on the other side. Climb up from the stream's ravine, then leave the main path to head right along the top of the rim, 100 feet out to the edge of the canyon. Here you'll have the best views yet: Mill Creek below and the entire mountain-bordered canyon stretching from east to west.

30 UPPER MILL CREEK SOUTH TO BLACK ROCK

Length: 26 miles round trip
Hiking time: 3 to 4 days
High point: 4,400 feet
Total elevation gain: 2,900 feet
Difficulty: moderate
Season: early May through November
Water: available from Mill Creek and other streams; purify first
Maps: USGS 7.5' Mineral, USGS 7.5' Onion Butte, USGS 7.5' Barkley Mountain
Permit: none required
Nearest campground: Hole in the Ground Campground
Information: Almanor Ranger District, Lassen National Forest

This trek is most attractive in late spring when whole hillsides erupt in a rainbow of flowers and water flows are highest. As you follow Mill Creek for a portion of its journey from Lassen Peak slopes to the Sacramento River, you'll have steep canyon walls, a diverse forest, and plenty of wildlife for company.

On Highway 36, go 9 miles east of Mineral (or 9 miles northwest of the junction of Highways 32 and 36) and turn south on Highway 172. Go 3 miles to the town of Mill Creek, then turn left onto a dirt road that's 0.3 mile past Mill Creek Resort. Stay straight at an intersection after 2.8 miles (a left soon leads to Hole in the Ground Campground); the trailhead is another 3.3 miles farther.

Douglas firs, incense cedars, and the occasional sugar pine comprise the forest as you make a 2.2-mile descent to the first glimpse of Mill Creek's surging waters. The trail then gently rises and falls along the slope, passing several small streams and numerous dogwood trees that sport large white flowers in spring.

Return to Mill Creek and the first good campsite at 4.5 miles. Climb again, then at 5.5 miles pass through a grove of California nutmeg trees, a rare plant that's easily identified by its sharp needles. At 6.5 miles, you'll cross a hillside where chaparral and wildflowers surround huge chunks of volcanic rock. This open area gives the first full views

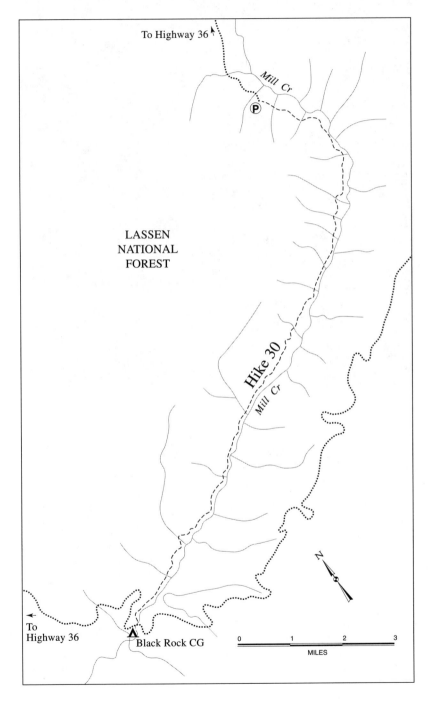

Blooming dogwoods add spring beauty to Mill Creek.

of the steep south side of the Mill Creek canyon and a better appreciation of Mill Creek's powers of erosion.

As you drop in elevation, ponderosa pines and black and canyon live
oaks dominate the forest. Reach the banks of Mill Creek and another
campsite at 8.1 miles. Follow the cold and clear waters for a level 1.7
miles past more campsites, then reach a flat at 10 miles that features
tall ponderosa pines.

The trail climbs from the flat to a verdant spring that emerges from
the dry slope. It then drops to a meadow where you'll find remnants of
an old orchard, easy access to Mill Creek, and level spots for camping.
Cross the meadow and travel the last mile below the imposing presence of Black Rock to Black Rock Campground, 13 miles from the
trailhead.

As described in hike 28, the trail continues farther west above Mill
Creek's north bank. See the trailhead directions for that hike if you
wish to be picked up at Black Rock Campground. For even more hiking, take hike 29 downstream on the south side of Mill Creek and west
of Black Rock.

31 ANTELOPE CREEK

Length: 12 miles round trip
Hiking time: 8 hours or 2 days
High point: 3,038 feet
Total elevation gain: 1,850 feet
Difficulty: moderate to strenuous
Season: mid-April through mid-November; weather permitting in winter
Water: available from Antelope Creek; purify first
Maps: USGS 7.5' Finley Butte, USGS 7.5' Panther Spring, USGS 7.5' Dewitt Peak
Permit: none required
Nearest campground: Battle Creek Campground
Information: Almanor Ranger District, Lassen National Forest

This journey holds a variety of visceral and spiritual delights year-round, but if you can, come in April and May when a thick rainbow of wildflowers clothes the hillsides and valleys, perfectly complementing the sweep of broad lava-rock canyon and the tumbling waters of Antelope Creek. You can do part of the hike in one day, but it's best to spend at least one night out here to fully appreciate the area's ambiance. Wear pants to help fend off poison oak; wear boots for better traction in muddy areas.

Take Highway 36 to Paynes Creek, go south on Paynes Creek Road for 0.3 mile, then turn right onto Plum Creek Road. Follow this paved road 7.2 miles, then turn right onto dirt High Trestle Road. Go 2.5 miles and park in the large open area just beyond Hogback Road.

Before beginning the hike, give your legs and lungs a good workout by climbing High Trestle Peak on the east side of the parking area. A steep

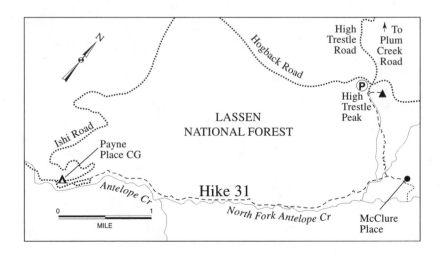

dirt road (which eventually turns into a narrow path) climbs 0.2 mile through mixed forest to the summit. Here you'll have the most far-ranging vista of the entire trek. The Trinities and Mount Shasta lie north, as do the Medicine Lake volcanoes, Magee Peak, Lassen Peak, and Brokeoff Mountain. To the west, the hills slope down to the Sacramento Valley, which eventually gives way to the distant peaks of the Coast Range. To the south, you'll see the North Fork Antelope Creek canyon, with farther mountains and canyons stretching south and east.

Back at the parking area, follow the dirt road downhill, staying straight along the seasonal creek when the road turns left and up, then descending on trail past chaparral and a variety of oaks. Cross a seasonal stream at 0.6 mile, then traverse an open slope studded with blue oaks that offers excellent views of the canyon rim. Cross another seasonal stream that's shaded by buckeyes and canyon live oaks at 1.6 miles, then continue slightly downhill to where the path levels in a meadow at 1.7 miles.

The meadow holds an unsigned trail fork. The main way heads downhill to the right. However, the left-hand trail makes an interesting side trip. It climbs 200 yards to McClure Place, an old ranching spot with fence posts, rock walls, and other human artifacts still in abundance (do not disturb them). Go 100 feet past the sign for McClure Place, then cross the small creek and skirt the south edge of the spring-fed meadow 200 yards to a saddle. Head down and to the right across an open slope for 100 yards, then walk straight down a steep

A backpacking family found this campsite near the banks of the North Fork Antelope Creek.

and grassy hillside to the banks of the North Fork Antelope Creek. Here you'll find two campsites nestled near the stream's cool and shaded waters. The flow of the creek, both here and farther downstream, is too fast to permit swimming.

The main path parallels a seasonal stream and then runs along an open, flower-filled hillside at 2.3 miles that allows good views of the canyon rim to the south. The path undulates as it travels past muddy areas and then descends to the first good, level camping areas by the North Fork Antelope Creek at 3.3 miles.

Continue up, along, and down the slope on the north side of the creek as you ramble through open oak forest and beside the beautiful stream's alder-bordered banks, passing more campsites and the occasional cow along the way. You'll eventually come to the confluence of the north and south forks of Antelope Creek, then reach the hike's official end at a barbed-wire fence and the border of the Tehama Wildlife Area at 6 miles.

If you want to do a one-way trip, follow the fence down toward Antelope Creek for 100 yards to Ishi Road, where you'll see a "trail" sign. This spot is on the east edge of a hairpin turn just north of Antelope Creek and 200 yards east of Payne Place Campground. Have your ride reach this spot from the trailhead by driving 2 miles west on Hogback Road, then continuing another 4 miles south on Ishi Road. Note that access into the Tehama Wildlife Area is prohibited from the first of December through the first Saturday in April and for three weeks during deer hunting season in and around October. Call (916) 597-2201 for more information about the Tehama Wildlife Area.

32 SPENCER MEADOW NATIONAL RECREATION TRAIL

Length: 13 miles round trip
Hiking time: 8 hours or 2 days
High point: 6,600 feet
Total elevation gain: 2,150 feet
Difficulty: moderate
Season: early May through late October
Water: available sporadically from creeks; purify first; bring your own
Maps: USGS 7.5' Childs Meadows, USGS 7.5' Reading Peak
Permit: none required
Nearest campground: Gurnsey Creek Campground
Information: Almanor Ranger District, Lassen National Forest

This journey takes you through dense stands of pine and fir, across green meadows large and small, and to the edge of a 50-foot waterfall. Since it begins at Highway 36 and tops out at 6,600 feet, it makes a

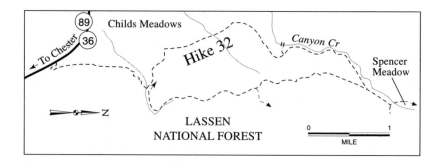

good warm-up backpacking trip in spring when snow smothers the other trails and trailheads in nearby Lassen Park.

The signed trailhead is a spacious parking area on the north side of Highway 36. It's 7.2 miles northwest of Highway 32, 4.8 miles east of Highway 89, and 0.3 mile east of the Childs Meadows Resort.

Travel 40 feet up the trail and look to the right for the first of dozens of National Recreation Trail emblems you'll see affixed to trees throughout the hike; this one is on an incense cedar. Continue up through a forest that also includes white fir, ponderosa pine, and occasionally a black oak. You'll also pass through some areas that are graced by the stately sugar pine; look on the ground and on the trees' upper branches for foot-long cones.

Cross a seasonal stream at 0.6 mile, then note tantalizing, tree-filtered glimpses of meadows and mountains that will later appear in full glory. A small spring flows slowly a few feet to the left of a switchback at 1.4 miles, followed by more forest and then a logged area at 1.8 miles with a small meadow, a seasonal stream, and a few level areas that could serve as mediocre campsites.

A trail fork awaits just beyond the seasonal stream. Bear left (the right fork is the return route) and continue through forest to the canyon overlook at 2.3 miles; here you can gaze far down to the emerald expanse of Childs Meadows and then west to the Mill Creek drainage and its surrounding mountains.

Continue along the undulating path past a spring-fed meadow to a magnificent northwesterly view of Lassen Park's Brokeoff Mountain and Mount Diller towering over the broad valley of Mill Creek. Contour around the mountainside and eventually hear the sound of rushing water at 5.4 miles. Turn left onto an unmarked side trail and walk briefly to the edge of the canyon, where you'll see the aptly named Canyon Creek plunge 50 feet over a precipice to further tumble down between steep walls.

Once you leave this magic spot and return to the main trail, climb gently through a forest that now includes red firs and western white pines, noting some level areas near the creek suitable for camping. Bear left at a trail fork at 6.8 miles, then ramble 0.2 mile up to Spencer Meadow. Ringed by lodgepoles and hosting a vast swath of green, the large meadow gives good views of Mount Conard to the northwest and the top portion of Lassen Peak just to the north. Look for campsites near the west and south edges.

When you're ready, head back 0.2 mile to the trail fork and go left. The way descends to border the west side of a meadow at 8.1 miles. Go right at a trail fork at 8.6 miles, cross another small meadow, then drop gently down along an open ridge to reach the hike's first trail fork at 11.2 miles. Bear left for the final 1.8 miles to the trailhead.

Canyon Creek has a placid birth in Spencer Meadow.

33 HEART LAKE NATIONAL RECREATION TRAIL

Length: 6 miles round trip
Hiking time: 4 hours or 2 days
High point: 6,550 feet
Total elevation gain: 1,000 feet
Difficulty: moderate
Season: late May through late October
Water: available from streams and Heart Lake; purify first
Maps: USGS 7.5' Grays Peak, USGS 7.5' Lassen Peak
Permit: none required
Nearest campground: Battle Creek Campground
Information: Hat Creek Ranger District, Lassen National Forest

Numerous meadows, melodious mountain streams, dense forest, and the reflection of Brokeoff Peak in Heart Lake's shallow waters are the highlights of this hike. It's best in late spring when you can let the several steep sections of trail help you get into shape for those longer, high-elevation summer backpacks. The best camping is at Heart Lake, but occasional level spots near the trail can serve in a pinch.

Take Forest Road 17, which leaves Highway 36 about 100 feet east of the Battle Creek bridge, 0.2 mile east of Battle Creek Campground, and 1 mile west of Lassen Park headquarters in Mineral. Go north for 9.6 miles (always follow signs for M17 and take the best road at forks), then cross the South Fork of Digger Creek. Look for the trailhead and the Heart Lake National Recreation Trail sign 100 feet farther.

Start the journey with the spicy scent of tobacco brush in your nostrils. After reaching the banks of the creek, climb through a mixed forest of white fir, incense cedar, and Jeffrey pine; near the first of several

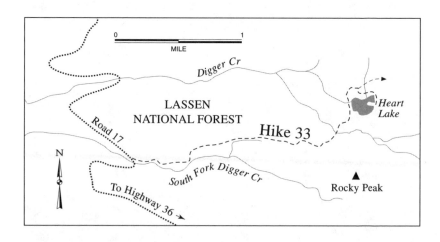

The west shore of Heart Lake

small meadows, a gargantuan sugar pine just to the right of the trail has dropped numerous foot-long cones.

Ascend past shaded springs and curve away from the creek, eventually reaching a small stream at 1.1 miles. Parallel it uphill past more verdant meadows filled with white, purple, and yellow flowers, noting at 1.5 miles the vibrant white bark and oscillating green leaves of quaking aspen near the stream. You'll soon spy a few lodgepoles near the water, and then welcome the appearance of stately red fir in the forest community.

Cross the creek and begin an even steeper climb. At 1.8 miles the path briefly levels; gaze between white firs for a westward glimpse of the Sacramento Valley and the Klamath Mountains. Give thanks when the path soon levels, allowing views filtered by western white pines of nearby Rocky Peak to the south and Brokeoff Mountain to the east.

Drop to a log crossing of a stream bordered by mountain alder at 2.1 miles, ascend briefly, run level through an area of downed trees, then drop again at 2.4 miles to the shores of Heart Lake, a broad and very shallow body of water dominated by Brokeoff Peak. This imposing member of Lassen Park royalty rises to a height of 9,235 feet, nearly 2,700 feet higher than the lake.

The path passes level areas suitable for camping on the west shore, then crosses the outlet (Digger Creek) to travel beside a small meadow. Bear right at a trail fork at 2.7 miles and bisect an especially beautiful meadow on the way to more campsites near the lake's eastern edge.

34 SPATTER CONE TRAIL

Length: 1.5 miles round trip
Hiking time: 2 hours
High point: 4,450 feet
Total elevation gain: 250 feet
Difficulty: easy to moderate
Season: mid-April through mid-November
Water: none; bring your own
Map: USGS 7.5' Old Station
Permit: none required
Nearest campground: Hat Creek Campground
Information: Hat Creek Ranger District, Lassen National Forest

About 30,000 years ago, fluid basalt from the region circumscribed by this loop trail flowed north, flooding the Hat Creek Valley for a distance of 16 miles and creating numerous lava tube caves such as nearby Subway Cave. This self-guided nature trail has a brochure (available at the trailhead) that details important aspects of natural history, especially volcanic geology. You'll explore several spatter cones and enjoy wide-ranging vistas of Lassen Peak and other nearby volcanic landforms.

To find the trailhead, reach Hat Creek Campground on Highway 89, 11.8 miles north of Lassen Park's north entrance and 1.4 miles south of the junction of Highways 89 and 44 East. Take the turnoff on the east side of 89 and park by the rest rooms.

The path climbs at the outset through a sparse forest of Jeffrey and ponderosa pines, then enters an open area dominated by greenleaf manzanita, mountain mahogany, antelopebrush, and sagebrush. Cross the Pacific Crest Trail at 0.2 mile, then turn left at a trail fork just beyond (you'll return via the right fork).

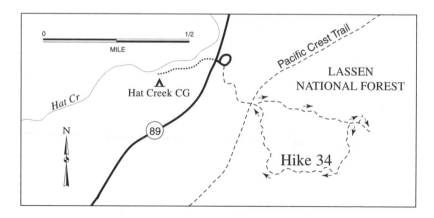

Sugarloaf Peak rises beyond the crater and rim of a spatter cone.

Reach the first of many large spatter cones at 0.7 mile near post 12. These spatter cones formed when vents spewed fountains of gaseous lava into the air. The chunks of hot lava flattened upon impact around the vents, forming the characteristic platy shells of rock. Be careful if you climb around the spatter cones: The unstable rock breaks easily. Do not dislodge any of the rock or collect samples.

The trail forks just beyond the first spatter cone, with a side trail going left to more spatter cones. From the highest of these, you'll have an excellent view of the surrounding volcanic terrain. West Prospect Peak rises to the southeast, with Lassen Peak and Chaos Crags dominating the entire landscape from a due-south vantage point. Lesser volcanoes lie west, while Sugarloaf Peak and its capping cinder cone attract the most attention to the northwest. The vast lava plains of the Hat Creek Valley run north, guarded by the Hat Creek Rim rising several hundred feet high on the east.

Return to the main loop to continue the hike. The path heads south past more spatter cones, then curves west. It eventually runs north, encounters even more spatter cones, then rejoins the lower portion of the loop near the Pacific Crest Trail.

35 SUBWAY CAVE TO HAT CREEK RIM

Length: 7.2 miles round trip
Hiking time: 5 hours or 2 days
High point: 4,900 feet
Total elevation gain: 600 feet
Difficulty: moderate
Season: mid-April through mid-November
Water: none; bring plenty
Map: USGS 7.5' Old Station
Permit: none required
Nearest campground: Cave Campground
Information: Hat Creek Ranger District, Lassen National Forest

This hike features two extremes: the close darkness of Subway Cave and the spacious brightness of Hat Creek Valley and the Hat Creek Rim. Subway Cave is always cool, but the ascent to the rim travels open territory that will drain your body moisture in summer heat. Take a sweater and two flashlights per person for the cave, and bring plenty of water and a hat for the climb.

Turn east off Highway 89 onto the Subway Cave access road, which is 0.3 mile north of the junction of Highways 89 and 44 East and across the road from Cave Campground. The parking area is 300 yards from the highway.

Begin with a subterranean journey through Subway Cave. This 1,300-foot-long lava tube formed about 30,000 years ago when large

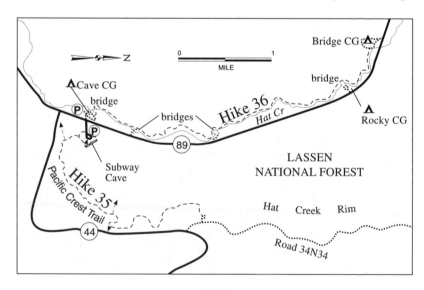

quantities of fluid basalt flowed north down the Hat Creek Valley. Lava on the surface cooled and hardened the fastest; hotter lava flowed farther before solidifying, thus forming the cave.

Lighted informational signs guide you through Stubtoe Hall, Black Grotto, Lucifer's Cul-de-Sac, and other features. Please refrain from making loud noises or damaging rock formations. For an interesting experience, find a dark part of the cave, turn off all lights, and then stand in silence for as long as you can.

Emerge from the cave at Rattlesnake Collapse and go left at a trail fork. Follow the wide path about 250 yards, then turn left onto an unsigned trail. You now pass through a flat area dominated by mountain mahogany, greenleaf manzanita, sagebrush, rabbitbrush, and antelope-brush, all chaparral plants adapted to the dry soil conditions that prevail in this section of Hat Creek Valley. Occasional western junipers and ponderosa and Jeffrey pines also dot the landscape.

Walk a level quarter mile, then turn left onto the Pacific Crest Trail. You'll follow this famous path for the rest of the hike; it's marked by colored ribbons beside and actually in the trail, and should be blazed in the near future.

Enjoy views of Prospect Peak and West Prospect Peak to the southeast and Sugarloaf Peak to the west as the PCT runs level for 1.2 miles, first east and then northeast, to a major fork. Bear right and continue to follow the ribbons, first past several stately sugar pines festooned with foot-long cones, then past a wide and level area on the left that is the best camping opportunity on the hike.

The view northwest from Hat Creek Rim: Hat Creek Valley, Freaner Peak, and Burney Mountain

The way now begins the climb up Hat Creek Rim and swings northerly through open forest. Leave the dirt road 0.7 mile past the just-mentioned major fork and go left on a path that heads uphill. There's no sign, but a large incense cedar stands on the right side of the road, and a small ponderosa pine with a blaze on its trunk and a juniper growing below is 10 feet up the path on the right. Ascend 0.3 mile to the rim and walk the needle-littered path past ponderosa and Jeffrey pines, incense cedars, western junipers, live oaks, and previously encountered chaparral shrubs.

Find an opening in the vegetation and get to the edge of the rim. From here, the Hat Creek Valley stretches north, with massive Mount Shasta in the distance. Burney Mountain reigns to the northwest, with Freaner Peak a few miles to the south. Sugarloaf Peak, due west, has large basalt flows near its base and a young cinder cone on its summit. Lassen Peak and Chaos Crags dominate the southern vista.

The path continues another 0.6 mile, then enters the west side of a PCT access point that has picnic tables and pit toilets. This is a good place to begin the hike, especially if you can arrange a car shuttle or only want the rim views. To reach it, drive Highway 44 east from its junction with Highway 89 for 2.7 miles, turn left onto Road 34N34, continue 0.3 mile, then turn left again onto Road 34N34F for the final 50 yards.

36 HAT CREEK

Length: 8.6 miles round trip
Hiking time: 5 hours
High point: 4,300 feet
Total elevation gain: 450 feet
Difficulty: easy
Season: early April through late November
Water: available from Hat Creek; purify first
Map: USGS 7.5' Old Station
Permit: none required
Nearest campground: Cave Campground
Information: Hat Creek Ranger District, Lassen National Forest

Map on page 98

Hat Creek begins as Lassen Peak snowmelt, then surges northward from Lassen Park through the Hat Creek Valley to merge with the Pit River at Lake Britton. This trail gives you good views of Lassen Peak, Mount Shasta, and other mountains, yet you'll always be near the crystal-clear stream. The creek tumbles through several small waterfalls and is nearly always turbulent enough for aural delight.

Take Highway 89 to Cave Campground, which is 0.3 mile north of the junction of Highways 89 and 44 East and across the road fom Subway

Two hikers watch the flowing waters of Hat Creek.

Cave (hike 35). Go 50 feet into the campground, then park in the small lot on the left.

Head north 100 yards and cross Hat Creek on a wooden bridge near a 5-foot waterfall. Turn right just beyond the bridge to begin the nearly level downstream stroll. Almost immediately on the right you'll see a sugar pine with its accompanying foot-long cones. Sugar pines are relatively rare on this hike, but you'll encounter plenty of western junipers, incense cedars, white firs, and ponderosa and Jeffrey pines. White alders line Hat Creek most of the way, usually towering above water-loving willows. The trail often passes through open territory thick with greenleaf manzanita, though you'll also see mountain mahogany, sagebrush, rabbitrabbit, and antelopebrush.

At 0.6 mile, a bridge leads to a spur road and Highway 89. Just beyond, follow your ears to a small waterfall dropping through a narrow gorge that's lined with grasses and moss. As you continue, note the views. Lassen Peak appears periodically behind you, while to the west Sugarloaf Peak stands over hillocks of basalt talus that stretch toward the creek. To the east, you'll note the Hat Creek Rim; over the last million years, the Hat Creek Valley separated from the Hat Creek Rim along a fault and slowly sank.

At 0.8 mile, look for a lone lodgepole pine beside the creek with some tobacco brush growing below it. This tree, recognized by its many small cones and two-needle bundles, usually grows only at higher elevations. At 1 mile, you'll reach the first of several aspen groves.

Another bridge at 1.7 miles again provides access to the east side of the creek and a spur road to Highway 89. Beyond the bridge, Mount Shasta soon appears to the north, with Burney Mountain to the northwest and Freaner Peak due west.

Reach two more small waterfalls at 2.2 and 2.4 miles as Hat Creek descends into a canyon that grows deeper as you progress northward. By 3.3 miles, you can see Crater and Magee Peaks in the Thousand Lakes Wilderness to the west; then the path descends along with the creek into a forest of pine, cedar, and fir that will provide shade and beauty the rest of the way.

At 3.7 miles, yet another wooden bridge crosses over to Rocky Campground and Highway 89. The path continues another 0.6 mile to end at the eastern edge of Bridge Campground. If you want to do a one-way trip, arrange to meet your ride here. Bridge Campground is 3.6 miles north of Cave Campground on the west side of Highway 89.

37 MAGEE PEAK

Length: 7 miles round trip
Hiking time: 6 hours or 2 days
High point: 8,550 feet
Total elevation gain: 3,200 feet
Difficulty: strenuous
Season: late June through October; some high elevation snow through July
Water: none; bring plenty
Maps: USGS 7.5' Jacks Backbone, USGS 7.5' Thousand Lakes Valley
Permit: none required
Nearest campground: Big Pine Campground
Information: Hat Creek Ranger District, Lassen National Forest

This trail is the steepest and most direct route to the soaring summit of Magee Peak. Part of an imposing volcano that towers above the upper reaches of the Sacramento Valley, Magee Peak commands a vast view over much of northwestern California. This hike connects with the paths

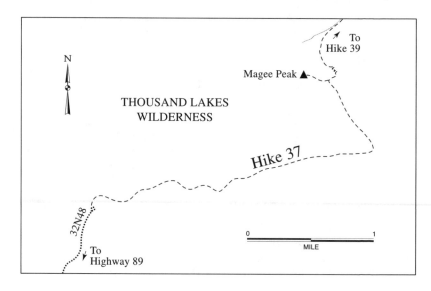

Lassen Peak and other Lassen Park volcanoes as viewed from the trail fork near the summit of Magee Peak

of hikes 38 and 39, allowing extensive exploration of the Thousand Lakes Wilderness; you can do a one-way trip by arranging to be picked up at either hike's trailhead. If you plan to camp on Magee Peak or nearby on the ridge, be prepared for high winds, and leave the heights if thunderstorms threaten (see the **Weather** section in the *Introduction*).

Get to the intersection of Road 16 and Highway 89, which is 4 miles north of the north entrance to Lassen Park and 9.5 miles south of the junctions of Highway 89 and Highway 44 East. Head up Road 16, staying on this main road at all intersections. After 10.1 miles, turn right onto Road 32N48 (50 yards past a left turn) and proceed 1.7 miles to the roomy trailhead.

The trail initially climbs gently northward past an understory of pinemat manzanita and huckleberry oak, the latter quickly replaced by bush chinquapin. The ascent steepens after 100 yards and a swing to the east. Tree branches part enough at 0.6 mile to allow a brief glimpse of the summit.

Continue upward through an open forest of Jeffrey pine, sugar pine, white fir, and red fir. You'll soon reach an elevation where winter conditions are too severe for sugar pine and white fir: The white fir drop away, while the closely related western white pine replaces its cousin, the sugar pine.

The path makes a 120-degree swing to the northwest at 2.5 miles and then leaves the forest shade at 2.7 miles to give the first good views. Let this sweep of space provide energy for your legs, lungs, and heart as you switchback ever upward past chaparral.

Reach the crest at 3.3 miles, where you'll see the trail heading down the other side to Magee and Everett lakes and the other attractions of hikes 38 and 39. From here, head west 0.2 mile amidst wind-whipped whitebark pines to the 8,549-foot summit of Magee Peak.

You now stand at the edge of a large composite volcano. Consisting of different types of lava erupted at different times, Magee Peak and environs are thus a geological cousin to Burney Mountain and Mount Shasta to the north and the ancient Mount Tehama to the southeast, the remnants of which include Brokeoff Mountain and the series of peaks stretching between it and Lassen Peak.

The vistas from this high-altitude vantage point stretch in every direction. Forests flow west toward the Sacramento River, with the far ridges of the Coast Range and Klamath Mountains beyond. Mount Shasta spikes skyward in isolated ivory splendor to the north. Near to the east, the glacially gouged Thousand Lakes Valley slopes gently down, bordered by steep cliffs. The Hat Creek Rim beckons farther to the east, while Lassen Peak and other Lassen Park landmarks dominate the southern skyline.

38 LAKE EILER LOOP

Length: 9.5 miles round trip
Hiking time: 7 hours or 2 days
High point: 6,500 feet
Total elevation gain: 650 feet
Difficulty: easy to moderate
Season: late June through October; many mosquitoes through July
Water: available from lakes and ponds; purify first
Map: USGS 7.5' Thousand Lakes Valley
Permit: none required
Nearest campground: Bridge Campground
Information: Hat Creek Ranger District, Lassen National Forest

The broad blue expanse of Lake Eiler highlights this easy walk into the watery heart of the Thousand Lakes Wilderness. Numerous lakes, reached by trail or cross-country, and the trails of hikes 37 and 39 beckon backcountry explorers. Note that four-wheel-drive vehicles usually can drive all the way to the actual trailhead, but since most hikers have two-wheel-drive vehicles, the hike description begins with the last 1.5 miles of road.

Reach Road 33N25, which is on Highway 89's west side, 1.2 miles south of Honn Campground, 7.4 miles north of 89's junction with Highway 44 East, and 50 yards north of Wilcox Road. Signs for Thousand Lakes Wilderness and Tamarack trailhead and/or wilderness placards on posts mark major junctions. Go straight at a three-way junction at 0.9 mile, then bear right at two major road forks at 1.2 and 2.2 miles. At 3.1 miles, Road 33N25 goes right and briefly joins Road 34N78 and then, after 50 yards, heads left uphill. Continue on 33N25, bear left at 4.5 miles, then reach Road 33N23Y at 6 miles, where you go right for the final 1.5 miles to the trailhead. Those with two-wheel-drive vehicles should park near this road fork.

The dirt road travels through a forest of white fir and Jeffrey pine, with an occasional lodgepole pine mixed in. Tobacco brush, manzanita, currant, bitter cherry, and spirea form the understory. Look south and east for open views of valley, forest, and mountains.

Reach the trailhead at 1.5 miles and exchange road for trail. Climb gently west for 0.8 mile, then head northwest through a shallow valley vibrant with currant, manzanita, bush chinquapin, and tobacco brush. Farther up, note the jumble of black basalt to the right as the trail bends west again.

Continue relatively level past small meadows lush with willow and spirea flower-spikes, then go right at a trail fork at 3.1 miles. Shortly beyond, you'll discover three shallow, trailside ponds ringed by lodgepole pines.

Ascend for another 0.4 mile, then drop to the shore of Lake Eiler, by far the largest body of water in the Thousand Lakes Wilderness.

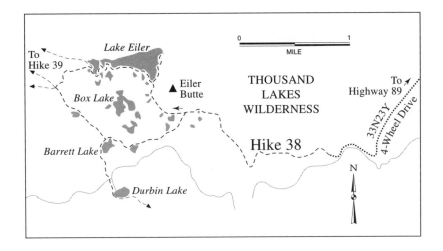

Lake Eiler and Freaner Peak

It's also one of the prettiest: From the grove of quaking aspen at the northeast edge, Lake Eiler reflects the imposing visage of Magee and Crater Peaks, Red Cliff, and the other thin-air heights that grace the southwestern horizon. Near the east, south, and west shores, backpackers will find numerous sites among a mixed forest composed of lodgepole, western white, and Jeffrey pines, and red and white firs. Warm-weather swimmers will find the steepest drop-offs along the south shore, which also offers the best views of the basalt boulder shoulders of Freaner Peak.

The main trail borders Lake Eiler's south side for 0.8 mile, then reaches a trail fork, where you go left. (A right turn takes you 2.3 miles to the hike 39 trailhead.) From here, climb gently 0.4 mile to a four-way junction. Going straight would connect you with hikes 37 and 39. However, bear left and hoof it 0.7 mile to lodgepole-lined Barrett Lake. Too shallow for swimming, the lake offers a campsite on the northwest side, an attractive option for those who find the much more popular Lake Eiler too crowded. For a similar milieu, head right at the trail fork for a half-mile side trip to Durbin Lake, which has more campsites.

To complete the loop from Barrett Lake, head northeast for a mile to the trail fork encountered east of Lake Eiler, turn right, and head back to the trailhead. Those with good cross-country hiking skills may instead want to investigate shallow Box Lake and the several ponds found in the interior of the loop.

39 EVERETT LAKE, MAGEE LAKE, AND MAGEE PEAK

Length: 12.6 miles round trip
Hiking time: 2 days
High point: 8,550 feet
Total elevation gain: 3,200 feet
Difficulty: moderate to strenuous
Season: late June through October; many mosquitoes and some high elevation snow through July
Water: available only at Twin, Everett, and Magee Lakes; purify first
Map: USGS 7.5' Thousand Lakes Valley
Permit: none required
Nearest campground: Bridge Campground
Information: Hat Creek Ranger District, Lassen National Forest

This trek takes you through vast stretches of virgin forest to two gorgeous subalpine lakes, then ends atop the windswept summit of Magee Peak, an isolated spot from which a great expanse of northern California spreads. Serious trekkers can undertake a thorough exploration of the Thousand Lakes Wilderness by walking the trails of hike 37 and hike 38. It also is possible to do a one-way hike by arranging to be picked up at the Magee Peak trailhead. If you camp on Magee Peak or nearby high ridges, expect high winds and be ready to skedaddle down into the forest if thunderstorms threaten (see the **Weather** section in the *Introduction* for precautions).

To reach the Cypress trailhead, your starting point, go west on Road 26, which leaves Highway 89 about 0.4 mile north of the Hat Creek

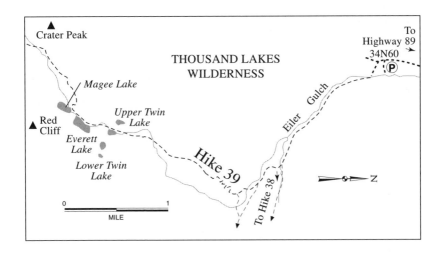

Magee Lake, one of the many beautiful bodies of water in the Thousand Lakes Wilderness

Work Center and 10 miles south of Highway 299. Travel Road 26 as it passes several lesser roads (follow signs for Road 26, Thousand Lakes Wilderness, and Cypress Camp) for 7.5 miles, then turn left onto Road 34N60. Take this road for the last 2.6 miles. A Thousand Lakes Wilderness Cypress Camp sign marks the parking area.

Begin the hike by heading up the dirt road. You'll reach two intersections within 200 yards: Go right at the first and left at the second. Your road quickly crosses Eiler Gulch, a seasonal stream that you'll hike near for the next 3 or so miles. The road turns to narrow track tread, passes a Cypress Trailhead sign, and begins a long, steady ascent. White fir and Jeffrey pine provide partial early morning and late afternoon shade for you and an understory of manzanita, bush chinquapin, and spice-scented tobacco brush.

Reach the boundary of Thousand Lakes Wilderness at 1.7 miles, then bear right at three trail forks over the next mile. A left at any of the three will take you to Lake Eiler and the trails of hike 38.

Continue a gentle climb through a forest of white and red firs and lodgepole and western white pines. The shallow waters of one of the Twin Lakes lies on the trail's left side at 4.2 miles. If you desire a summer swim, head 300 yards southeast to the deeper waters of another Twin Lake.

Push 0.3 mile to Everett Lake, a large and deep body of water bordered by forest and guarded by the steep slopes of Red Cliff. Everett Lake offers shoreline views of Magee and Crater peaks and the rest of the upper section of the Thousand Lakes Valley. Look for campsites above the lake on the east and southeast sides. Nearby Magee Lake shares similar characteristics and views as sibling Everett but has many more campsites sprinkled around its circumference.

From Magee Lake, the trail steepens as it ascends southwest to the ridge, first through a forest of stately red firs and then, higher up, through more open stands of hardier mountain hemlocks and western white pines. As your breathing accelerates from the climb, let your eyes roam from the many hues of the volcanic rock at your feet to the ever-expanding views of the Thousand Lakes Valley.

Reach the ridge crest at 6.3 miles, then pause to admire the scenery, catch your breath, and note the trail heading downhill (hike 37). Continue on the faint path to the right 0.3 mile to the crest of 8,549-foot Magee Peak. As you survey the volcano's semicircular rim, note Crater Peak (8,683 feet) just to the north and another peak (8,446 feet) to the east. The entire rim cradles the glacially carved Thousand Lakes Valley.

But the highlight is the panorama over northern California. Lassen Peak and its nearest neighbors dominate the southeast. Sloping forests lead down to the Sacramento Valley to the west, with the Coast Range on the horizon to the southwest. Guide your eye along the Klamath Mountains to the snowy summit of Mount Shasta in the north. Fall River Valley and volcanic mountains stretch northeast beyond the Hat Creek Rim.

40 CRYSTAL AND BAUM LAKES

Length: up to 5 miles round trip
Hiking time: 3 hours
High point: 3,000 feet
Total elevation gain: 50 feet
Difficulty: easy
Season: year-round; occasional winter snow
Water: available from lakes; purify first
Map: USGS 7.5' Cassel
Permit: none required
Nearest campground: Cassel Campground
Information: Recreation Department, PG&E

This hike has many attractions: level walking beside two beautiful lakes, water-reflected views of Burney Mountain and Mount Shasta, fishing for brown and rainbow trout, and excellent bird-watching, especially for hawks, osprey, and migratory geese and ducks. Consider combining it with hike 41 for a one-way walk by having someone meet you at the hike 41 trailhead.

From the intersection of Highways 89 and 299, drive 299 east 2 miles, then turn south onto Cassel Road. Go 2 more miles, turn left when you see the sign for Crystal Lake Fish Hatchery, go another mile, then turn left into the parking area. If coming north on Highway 89, take Cassel Road, travel 3 miles to Cassel, continue west and north 2 more miles, then turn right for the final mile to the parking area.

From the parking area, head over to the dam that separates the two lakes. The hike around Crystal Lake heads west (left) from the north side of the dam. An occasionally muddy 2-mile path circles most of the shoreline. You'll travel past Oregon white oak, black oak, western juniper, and squawbush on the north side and then walk through an open ponderosa pine forest on the south side. Note that a fence near the south side of the dam will force you to return to the parking area on the road. Highlights include southwest views of Burney Mountain, northwest views of Mount Shasta's snowy slopes, and good opportunities to observe geese, ducks, and occasionally white pelicans on and above the lake's far reaches.

The 1.5-mile path along Baum Lake's west shore (which includes a portion of the Pacific Crest Trail) also begins at the north side of the dam. Go right, then follow the obvious path north. Ponderosa pines grow near the shore, with oaks dominating the slope to the left.

The way soon splits. The lower trail runs along the shore. The upper trail travels mid-slope, crosses a fence, then reaches another fork. The Pacific Crest Trail heads left and uphill; you stay right and eventually meet the lower trail. Continue along the leaf-littered path past lava-rock talus, negotiate a brushy area near a small creek, then reach Baum Lake Dam. If you desire more hiking, take a trail from the east side of the dam 400 yards down to Hat Creek's banks, or walk south along the canal that travels to Hat 2 Powerhouse on the west side of Hat Creek (see hike 41).

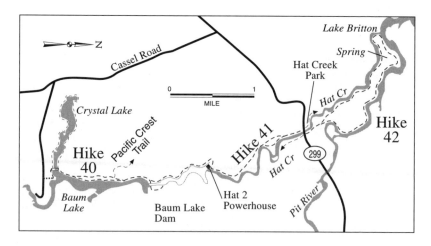

Twilight glows on the still surface of Crystal Lake.

41 HAT CREEK TO BAUM LAKE DAM

Length: 5 miles round trip
Hiking time: 3 hours
High point: 3,000 feet
Total elevation gain: 200 feet
Difficulty: moderate
Season: year-round; occasional winter snow
Water: available from Hat Creek; purify first
Map: USGS 7.5' Cassel
Permit: none required
Nearest campground: Pit River Campground
Information: Recreation Department, PG&E

Map on page 110

Hat Creek has a special beauty: Its cold and clear waters flow swiftly between its wide banks, and the accompanying lush growth of bordering green sharply contrasts with the sparse and dry vegetation that covers nearby mountains and fields. This trail, popular with those who pursue trout, offers the hiker a variety of scenery and the opportunity to observe firsthand how PG&E generates electricity from the creek. Note that the trail occasionally fades, although the general direction is obvious; stay within 100 yards of Hat Creek the whole way to Hat 2 Powerhouse. It's possible to combine this hike with hike 40 for a one-way trip. Have your ride meet you at the hike 40 trailhead.

Hat Creek Park is a family favorite for picnics and toe dipping.

Reach Hat Creek Park, which is on the north side of Highway 299, about 4 miles east of the 89/299 junction and 5 miles west of Fall River Mills.

Cross Highway 299 and the fence on the west side of the Hat Creek bridge. Travel south through a ponderosa pine forest, then reach an open area at 0.3 mile that allows you to see nearby volcanic landforms.

Continue to a trail fork at 0.5 mile. Take either route; they rejoin a few hundred yards farther upstream. Once the two paths merge, continue on to the Hat 2 Powerhouse parking lot at 1.6 miles. (If you wish to drive here, take the road that heads south from Highway 299 about 1 mile west of Hat Creek Park.)

From the downstream side of the powerhouse, head uphill on either side of the large pipe to a canal. The canal brings Hat Creek water from Baum Lake Dam to this point, where it travels through the pipe to rotate turbines and thus produce electricity.

After you've caught your breath, stroll southerly along either side of the canal. As you continue to Baum Lake Dam, views include Hat Creek, Soldier Mountain, Saddle Mountain, and many other peaks and ridges.

Reach the dam and the northern edge of Baum Lake at 2.5 miles. Here you'll note that most of the water enters the canal, but some surges north down the valley. Look for a trail on the east side of the dam that drops 0.25 mile to Hat Creek's banks. To do hike 40, head to the west shore of Baum Lake and walk south.

Nearby: For another hiking option from Hat Creek Park, follow the dirt road 1.4 miles south along Hat Creek's east side to a point opposite the Hat 2 Powerhouse.

42 HAT CREEK/PIT RIVER CONFLUENCE

Length: 3.1 miles round trip
Hiking time: 2 hours
High point: 2,800 feet
Total elevation gain: 100 feet
Difficulty: easy
Season: year-round; occasional winter snow
Water: available from Hat Creek; purify first
Map: USGS 7.5' Cassel
Permit: none required
Nearest campground: Pit River Campground
Information: Recreation Department, PG&E

Map on page 110

The Hat Creek/Pit River peninsula swarms with wildlife, especially birds. The reason is that it has riparian habitat, marshlands, oak forest, and open meadow, each of which is favored by different birds. Look

Winter-bare Oregon white oaks above the swollen Pit River

and listen for water ouzels, red-winged blackbirds, Steller's jays, great blue herons, redtailed hawks, bald eagles, and a variety of geese and ducks (especially prevalent in winter and spring). Anglers ply Hat Creek's waters for trout, but most stay close to Highway 299.

Find the trailhead at Hat Creek Park, which is on the north side of Highway 299, about 4 miles east of the 89/299 junction and 5 miles west of Fall River Mills.

Walk to the far (east) side of the Highway 299 bridge and go left (north) on the dirt road. The road initially travels past diatomite, a white, powdery substance. Diatomite is composed of the fossilized remains of the silica-containing shells of organisms that lived in an ancient lake that once covered this area.

You immediately gain a ridge and travel through an open forest of black and Oregon white oak that frames left-side views of Hat Creek's serene waters and right-side views of a marsh and the Pit River. At 0.2 mile, a faint road heads right; this is your return route.

The dirt road on the left heads northwest through a meadow dotted with blue oaks and tall ponderosa pines, with views of Mount Shasta directly ahead. As you continue, note the old fruit trees, remnants of long-gone homesteaders who made this beautiful area home.

At 1.4 miles, you'll reach the edge of the peninsula where Hat Creek and the Pit River meet at Lake Britton's southeast edge. After enjoying the view of the water rimmed by low mountains, head northeast and catch a faint path that travels near the bluff overlooking the Pit River. You'll soon reach a spring sheltered by white alders, Oregon white oak, and a ponderosa pine. Its shallow pool emits a stream that flows down to Lake Britton. The mighty Pit River accompanies you the rest of the way back to the trailhead.

Nearby: Three other trails leave from Hat Creek Park. One runs northwest through forest for 1.6 miles on Hat Creek's west side to reach Lake Britton. Another hugs Hat Creek's east bank and runs southeast for 1.4 miles. The third, described in hike 41, travels open areas near Hat Creek's west bank southeast to the Hat 2 Powerhouse and beyond to Baum Lake. All three trails are on PG&E land.

43 BURNEY FALLS

Length: 4.9 miles round trip
Hiking time: 3 hours, day hike only
High point: 3,000 feet
Total elevation gain: 300 feet
Difficulty: easy
Season: year-round; occasional winter snow
Water: available in the campground and near the Visitor's Information Center
Map: USGS 7.5' Burney Falls
Permit: none required
Nearest campground: McArthur-Burney Falls Memorial State Park Campground
Information: McArthur-Burney Falls Memorial State Park

A huge underground reservoir delivers 100 million gallons of water daily to the lip of Burney Falls. From here, the water surges white as it drops 129 feet to crash into a deep sapphire pool. The Falls Trail, a 1-mile loop, takes you near both the base and the crest of the falls and serves as the hub for three other trails.

Burney Falls thunders into a large and deep pool.

Reach the intersection of Highways 299 and 89, go 6 miles north on Highway 89, then turn left and follow the signs for McArthur-Burney Falls Memorial State Park. Drive past the check-in station and park in the lot.

Buy the Falls Trail brochure, a handy guide that describes the natural history of the area, then head over to the Falls Overlook for the first view of the massive cascade. When you're ready, follow the paved

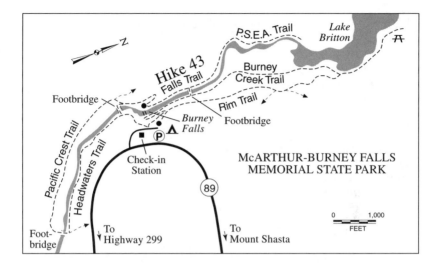

path down to creekside. A short side path takes you 100 yards to the edge of the broad pool. Here sheets of mist from the base of the falls bring soothing moisture to bare skin.

Continue along the main path past huge chunks of basalt talus that fell from the cliff rim above. The Falls Trail soon turns left to cross Burney Creek. However, stay straight and begin the Burney Creek Trail. Walk well away from the creek through an open forest of Douglas fir, ponderosa pine, incense cedar, black oak, and Oregon white oak. Go left after a half mile at a trail fork (a right on the Rim Trail takes you to the campground and back to the Falls Overlook). Continue another 0.3 mile to a picnic area and swimming beach at Lake Britton, whose waters are much warmer than frigid Burney Creek.

Head back to the Falls Trail, cross the bridge, then turn right onto the P.S.E.A. Trail. This path travels very near Burney Creek and takes you past white alder, dogwood, and Douglas fir to end at a gate. Look for several creekside spots where you can rest and watch the water flow.

Return to the Falls Trail and follow it upstream and uphill as you enjoy views of the falls, Burney Creek canyon, and the tops of Douglas firs. Upon reaching a trail fork, turn right and then left. You're on the Pacific Crest Trail, which you follow 0.7 mile to a bridge across Burney Creek. Relatively little water flows here; most enters from springs farther downstream.

Turn left onto the Headwaters Trail just beyond the bridge. You now make a half-mile jaunt near the creek banks, ending at a trail fork near the top of the falls. Go left to the middle of the bridge, from which you can see the swift stream preparing to plunge off the precipice. When you're ready to leave this power spot, return to the trail fork and bear left for the final 150 yards to the parking lot.

44   PIT RIVER FALLS

Length: 2.6 miles round trip
Hiking time: 2 hours
High point: 3,350 feet
Total elevation gain: 400 feet
Difficulty: strenuous
Season: year-round; some winter snow
Water: available from Pit River; purify first
Map: USGS 7.5' Hogback Ridge
Permit: none required
Nearest campground: Pit River Campground
Information: Recreation Department, PG&E

The Pit River begins high in the Warner Mountains of California's extreme northeast corner. It snakes south and west through the volcanic landscape of the Modoc Plateau and Cascades and then dissolves

Pit River Falls rumbles through a 300-foot-deep canyon.

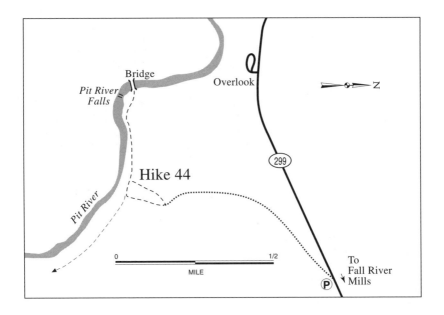

into the vastness of Shasta Lake. Along the way, humans use its waters for agriculture and power generation. This hike takes you to Pit River Falls, a wide and raucous 30-foot tumble, which lies in the bottom of a 300-foot-deep canyon out of sight of ranches and PG&E powerhouses. But you'll have to work to gain the falls' splendor by making a steep and rough descent (and return ascent) through brushy terrain—wear pants and boots.

Drive Highway 299 east from Highway 89 and Hat Creek, then turn into a wide parking area on the south side of the road that is a half mile east of the vista point (a great place to see your destination), a mile west of Fall River Mills, and right next to a Welcome to Fall River sign.

Start the hike on the dirt road that heads west and then south from the parking area (four-wheelers and other high-clearance vehicles can take it to the edge of the canyon). The road runs flat past rabbitbrush, buckbrush, western juniper, and gray and ponderosa pines.

At 0.5 mile, you'll reach the canyon. Pause here to gather in the view: At 7,863 feet, Burney Mountain dominates the entire landscape from the southwest; Hanley Mountain rises to the northwest on the other side of Highway 299; due south is Hogback Ridge; and just below is the Pit River coursing through its canyon, with redtailed hawks, turkey vultures, and an occasional golden eagle soaring on spread wings in and above the chasm.

Two faint and unmarked paths wind down to the floor of the canyon. Take the one on the right: It avoids most of the poison oak and squawbush thickets. Note the rock layers as you pick your way down; they're due to successive eruptions of basalt.

You'll be glad to reach the bottom of the canyon, where you head downstream past redbud, squawbush, and Oregon white oak on the Winters Toll Road. This historic dirt road, traveled as early as 1859, was once the main thoroughfare connecting Fall River Valley with major destinations to the west.

As you near the falls, your skin tingles and your ears fill with the thunderous roar. It's fairly easy to explore near the base and lip of the falls, and strong swimmers will find a deep spot with relatively slow current about 100 feet downstream. You'll also see the remains of an iron bridge below the falls. Stay off: It's missing much of its flooring.

45 BIG LAKE AND HORR POND

Length: up to 8 miles round trip
Hiking time: 4 hours
High point: 3,300 feet
Total elevation gain: none
Difficulty: easy
Season: late April through mid-November; other times when weather and road conditions permit; hunting season runs from early October to mid-January
Water: available from Big Lake, Horr Pond, and the Tule River; purify first
Map: USGS 7.5' Fall River Mills
Permit: none required
Nearest campground: Pit River Campground
Information: Recreation Department, PG&E

This level levee walk features a full range of sensual delights: the smell and taste of fresh mountain air tinged with tangy juniper scent; the feel of the wind bringing cool water vapor to the cheek; the sound of Canada geese, mallards, and redtailed hawks calling out to each other and the world; the sight of volcanoes—far and near, large and small—ringing the Fall River Valley.

Drive Highway 299 to the Fall River Valley and the small town of McArthur. Go north on Main Street past the fairgrounds to a dirt road. At 0.5 mile, go right and pass through a gate. The dirt road continues north another 3 miles to the parking area. Note that winter rains can make four-wheel drive a necessity, though PG&E grades the road to passable two-wheel drive in late April or May.

As you explore the shores of Big Lake and Horr Pond, the large number and variety of birds will astound you. Through the middle of spring, the area hosts large numbers of migratory birds that feed in nearby fields (such as Hollenbeck Swamp just south of Big Lake). The sudden rise of a thousand snow geese, accompanied by a chaotic chorus of high-pitched cries, can be the high point of your day, or your year. Many other species are winter/spring or year-round residents, including Canada

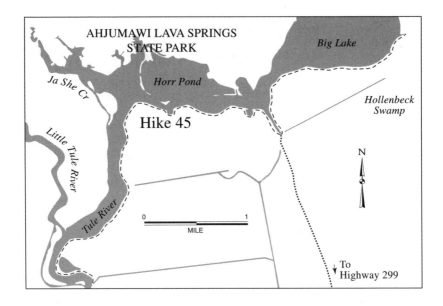

goose, cackling goose, Pacific white-fronted goose, cinnamon teal, green-winged teal, northern pintail, and northern shoveler. You'll also see numerous great blue herons and quite possibly some osprey. If you're lucky, you'll spot the relatively rare white pelican or greater sandhill crane.

You have two hiking options. The first leaves along the right-hand side of the narrow water channel by the parking area and initially heads north towards Ahjumawi Lava Springs State Park, the home of hikes 46 through 48. The path soon bends east to hug the southern shore of Big Lake for a mile. Like many of the rivers and lakes in the Fall River Valley, Big Lake and Horr Pond owe their existence to the porous lava rock that makes up much of the Modoc Plateau of northeastern California. Water from the Tule Lake region 50 miles to the north travels underground to emerge here.

The left-hand trail leaves the parking area to run north and then west for over a mile along the shore of Horr Pond. Here you have unimpeded views of Mount Shasta's snowy crown to the northwest, Soldier Mountain topping the western edge of the Fall River Valley, and a string of massive volcanoes stretching south from Burney Mountain to Crater and Magee Peaks and then to Lassen Peak and Chaos Crags. The levee soon curves south to travel nearly 2 miles along the banks of the Tule River. Now, in addition to having the mountain views, you'll see pastoral settings of barn and field, reminders of the broad valley's fertility.

46 CRYSTAL SPRINGS AND JA SHE CREEK

Length: 5.4 miles round trip
Hiking time: 3 hours
High point: 3,325 feet
Total elevation gain: 100 feet
Difficulty: easy
Season: late April through mid-November; other times when weather and road conditions permit; hunting season runs from early October to mid-January
Water: available from Horr Pond and Ja She Creek; purify first
Map: USGS 7.5' Fall River Mills
Permit: none required
Nearest campground: three campsites at Horr Pond, three each at nearby Crystal Springs and Ja She Creek; camping forbidden elsewhere in the park
Information: McArthur-Burney Falls Memorial State Park

This journey features a full complement of natural and human history: The southern horizon holds Lassen Park peaks and other nearby mountains; Horr Pond hosts a plethora of water birds, including Canada geese, mallards, teals, pelicans, great blue herons, and ospreys; water from 50 miles north seeps underground through porous volcanic rock to emerge at Crystal Springs; Crystal Springs is also the site of rock fish traps used by the Ajumawi Indians; and at the hike's far point is an old farm. Note that you'll have to boat to the trailhead (see next paragraph).

Drive Highway 299 to the Fall River Valley and the small town of McArthur. Go north on Main Street past the fairgrounds to a dirt road. At 0.5 mile, go right and pass through a gate. The dirt road continues north another 3 miles to the parking area. Note that winter rains can make four-wheel drive a necessity, though PG&E grades the road to passable two-wheel drive in late April or May. Ready your kayak, canoe, or other watercraft and head north out the narrow channel (be sure to follow all proper precautions for safe water travel). Once beyond the channel, travel a mile northwest toward Mount Shasta, then land at the Horr Pond camping area (look for trash cans near the shore). Motorboats must bypass Horr Pond and travel to the deeper landing area at Crystal Springs another mile west.

Start the hike by heading west from the Horr Pond campsites on the Lava Springs Trail. Stay near the water's edge as you watch the waterbirds work and play in front of Prospect Peak, West Prospect Peak, Lassen Peak, Chaos Crags, Thousand Lakes Wilderness summits, and Burney Mountain. Bear left at a trail fork at 0.6 mile, then spy a small, marshy pond on the right. Pass lava boulder fields and western juniper trees, then note a large ponderosa pine that splits into three trunks.

You'll soon reach the first of three environmental campsites at Crystal

Crystal Springs gently enters Ja She Creek.

Springs and then Crystal Springs itself at 1.2 miles. From this placid place of beauty, you can see the water flowing under oak branches into lower Ja She Creek. The Ajumawi Indians built the rock fish traps

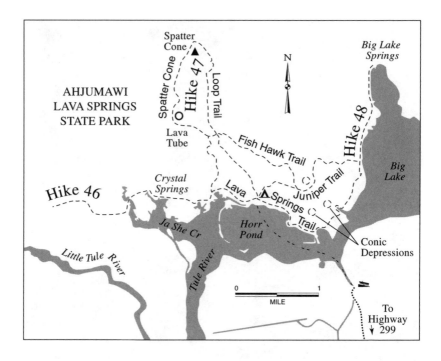

surrounding the springs; *Lat he*—Sacramento sucker fish—come here to spawn in the spring, when the Ajumawi would close off the route back to Ja She Creek with rocks to catch the fish. A signboard provides more details about the Ajumawi; another displays a map of the park. The area also has a small building that could serve as a shelter in an emergency.

The path then wanders away from the shoreline to travel past lava flows, eventually reaching and crossing upper Ja She Creek at 1.7 miles. From the bridge spanning the stream, you can peer into the clear waters; if you desire a swim, try the waist-high water on the downstream, eastern side of the bridge. Another signboard describes the natural history of Ja She Creek.

The route soon leaves the water behind and travels through open country past three more campsites. Fields and large barns in the distance give picturesque testimony of the Fall River Valley's agricultural economy.

Enter ponderosa pine forest at 2.2 miles. More meadows follow, with a large one stretching north to an old homestead site. From here, you'll also have the first full view of distant Mount Shasta. The path eventually bridges a small brook, then ends at another abandoned farm—a two-story farmhouse surrounded by an old barn and several outbuildings.

47 SPATTER CONE LOOP TRAIL

Length: 4.9-mile loop
Hiking time: 3 hours
High point: 3,470 feet
Total elevation gain: 250 feet
Difficulty: easy to moderate
Season: late April through mid-November; other times when weather and road
   conditions permit; hunting season runs from early October to mid-January
Water: available from Horr Pond at the beginning of the hike; purify first
Maps: USGS 7.5' Fall River Mills, USGS 7.5' Timbered Crater
Permit: none required
Nearest campground: three campsites at Horr Pond, three each at nearby
   Crystal Springs and Ja She Creek; camping forbidden elsewhere in the park
Information: McArthur-Burney Falls Memorial State Park

Map on page 124

Volcanoes and volcanic activity highlight this hike: In the distance, majestic Mount Shasta rises high to the northwest, and Lassen Peak and nearby monster summits dominate the skyline to the south; up close, you can enter a lava tube cave and clamber along the rim of a spatter cone. Most of the terrain along the route is open and bordered by hills of basaltic rock deposited in chaotic jumbles. Stark and beautiful but not the most hospitable during the heat: Do this one on a cool day or

Exploring a lava tube cave near the Spatter Cone Loop Trail

in the morning. Note that you'll have to boat to the trailhead (see next paragraph).

Drive Highway 299 to the Fall River Valley and the small town of McArthur. Go north on Main Street past the fairgrounds to a dirt road. At 0.5 mile, go right and pass through a gate. The dirt road continues north another 3 miles to the parking area. Note that winter rains can make four-wheel drive a necessity, though PG&E grades the road to passable two-wheel drive in late April or May. Ready your kayak, canoe, or other watercraft and head north out the narrow channel (be sure to follow all proper safety precautions for safe water travel). Once beyond the channel, travel a mile northwest toward Mount Shasta, then land at the Horr Pond camping area (look for trash cans near the shore). Motorboats must bypass Horr Pond and travel to the deeper landing area at Crystal Springs another mile west.

From the campsites at Horr Pond, head west near the shore on the Lava Springs Trail, quickly passing a right-forking trail, your return route. Near the water, a variety of birds go about the daily activities of their lives; year-round residents include Canada geese, great blue herons, mallards, osprey, and cinnamon teals. Beyond the stretch of shallow water, you'll spy Prospect and West Prospect peaks, Lassen Peak, Chaos Crags, and the thin-air summits in Thousand Lakes Wilderness.

Note a small spring seeping from the porous volcanic rock at the water's edge just before you reach a trail fork at 0.6 mile. Bear right onto the Spatter Cone Loop Trail and walk north, initially through a sparse forest of western juniper, ponderosa pine, and white and black oak. Soon you enter the surreal realm of lava land, where the bare, black basalt forms a brooding landscape. You, however, have the relatively smooth trail to guide you comfortably on.

Obtain the first tree-filtered view of Mount Shasta at 1.4 miles. As you continue up, stop occasionally to take in the southern view gained during your earlier wandering near the water. At 1.6 miles stay left at a fork (a right goes 0.2 mile to the other side of the loop), then note several large, mountain mahoganies growing beside the trail.

Look for a sign on the right at 2.1 miles. Just beyond it waits a small cave, the remnant of a lava tube created thousands of years ago. Lava tubes form from flows of liquid basalt. The lava near the surface of the flow cools first, while the hotter and more fluid liquid lava below streams out from underneath, leaving a hollow tube behind. The cave, about 15 feet wide, 30 feet deep, and up to 6 feet high, provides a cool respite when it is hot above. You won't need a light to explore it, but be careful: The floor is uneven and you can easily bump your head.

Leave the cave and climb moderately, soon reaching the first full view of Mount Shasta. A small mountain of lava rises to the right; curve easterly around it, then reach the spatter cone just to the right of the trail at 3.0 miles. Climb the rim to gain the full view of the spatter cone, which measures 100 feet across and 20 feet deep. Spatter cones form when volcanic vents shoot fountains of gaseous lava skyward; the hot lava falls around the vent to flatten on impact, thus forming platelike layers of thin and brittle rock that can make for tricky walking.

From the spatter cone, start a long and gentle southern descent featuring a panorama of Lassen Peak and other mountains. Reach the connector trail to the other side of the loop at 4.1 miles. Go left, continue another 100 yards, then bear right at another trail fork (a left takes you 1 mile on the Fish Hawk Trail to hike 48's Juniper Trail). From here, it's an easy 0.8 mile back to the hike's beginning at the Horr Pond campsites.

48 BIG LAKE SPRINGS

Length: 5.4 miles round trip
Hiking time: 3 hours
High point: 3,425 feet
Total elevation gain: 200 feet
Difficulty: easy
Season: late April through mid-November; other times when weather and road conditions permit; hunting season runs from early October to mid-January
Water: available from Horr Pond and Big Lake; purify first
Maps: USGS 7.5' Fall River Mills, USGS 7.5' Timbered Crater
Permit: none required
Nearest campground: three campsites at Horr Pond, three each at nearby Crystal Springs and Ja She Creek; camping forbidden elsewhere in the park
Information: McArthur-Burney Falls Memorial State Park

Map on page 124

The hike to Big Lake Springs travels a 3-mile stretch along the shores of Horr Pond and Big Lake, allowing you to observe geese, ducks, herons, and a large variety of other waterbirds and also to have unimpeded southward views of valley and mountain that stretch all

Big Lake Springs: a calm and peaceful spot (Photo by Rick Ramos)

the way to Lassen Park. Note that you'll have to boat to the trailhead (see next paragraph).

Drive Highway 299 to the Fall River Valley and the small town of McArthur. Go north on Main Street past the fairgrounds to a dirt road. At 0.5 mile, go right and pass through a gate. The dirt road continues north another 3 miles to the parking area. Note that winter rains can make four-wheel drive a necessity, though PG&E grades the road to passable two-wheel drive in late April or May. Ready your kayak, canoe, or other watercraft and head north out the narrow channel (be sure to follow all proper safety precautions for safe water travel). Once beyond the channel, travel a mile northwest toward Mount Shasta, and then land at the Horr Pond camping area (look for trash cans near the shore). Motorboats must bypass Horr Pond and travel to the deeper landing area at Crystal Springs another mile west.

From the Horr Pond campsites, head easterly along the shore of Horr Pond on Lava Springs Trail and enjoy panoramic views of Prospect Peak, West Prospect Peak, Lassen Peak, Chaos Crags, Thousand Lakes Wilderness mountains, Burney Mountain, and Soldier Mountain. Directly to the east, Big Valley Mountain rises steeply above the Fall River Valley. Its western edge marks the boundary of a fault, along which Big Valley Mountain rose over the eons as Fall River Valley dropped, a geological pattern that marks much of the terrain of northeastern California, southeastern California, western Utah, and Nevada.

At about 1 mile, the trail ascends a small rise at the east end of Horr Pond to reveal a sweeping vista of Big Lake. It then turns north along the lake.

Western juniper, occasional groves of black and Oregon white oak, and willows provide pleasant company as you continue. Reach a small cove at 1.4 miles that's a favorite sunning spot for turtles, then walk briefly uphill to see a large conic depression that holds a small pond.

Go straight at a trail fork at 1.9 miles, then note the several large ponderosa pines that grace the route. Continue past chunky lava flows and more ponderosa pines as you alternate between the shore of Big Lake and its hilly, bordering terrain.

Pass through a small, open thicket at 2.9 miles to reach Big Lake Springs. Here you can sit in the green grass and watch the spring's small flow merge with the vast stillness of Big Lake. The water originates as rain and snow melt in the vicinity of Tule Lake 50 miles north; it slowly percolates through porous basalt lava to form this spring and most, if not all, of the other springs in the Fall River Valley, including the springs that form Fall River itself.

When you're tanned, rested, and ready, leave Big Lake Springs and head back the way you came, 1 mile to a trail fork, where you head right on the Juniper Trail. Climb through mixed forest, stay right on the wide main path at an unmarked junction 0.8 mile farther, then note a second conic depression on the right that looks like a large meteor crater. Continue 0.2 mile to a trail fork (watch closely for the trail before and after). The Fish Hawk Trail goes right for 1 mile to meet the Spatter Cone Loop Trail and hike 47. You go left for a half-mile ramble to the Horr Pond campsites and the hike's end.

MOUNT SHASTA WILDERNESS

Corn lilies, water, and the lush expanse of lower Squaw Meadows

49   GRAY BUTTE

Length: 3.4 miles round trip
Hiking time: 2 hours
High point: 8,119 feet
Total elevation gain: 750 feet
Difficulty: moderate
Season: late June through October
Water: bring your own
Maps: USGS 7.5' McCloud, USFS Mt. Shasta Wilderness
Permit: required; available just beyond Panther Meadows for day hikes;
obtain from Mount Shasta Ranger District or McCloud Ranger District for
overnight trips; dogs prohibited
Nearest campground: Panther Meadows Campground
Information: Mount Shasta Ranger District, Shasta-Trinity National Forest

This hike takes you to the summit of Gray Butte, a peak just 4 crow
miles due south of Mount Shasta's summit. But even though you're
6,000 feet lower, you'll have similar views, the panorama lacking only
the vista that's blocked by mighty Shasta's girth. As an added bonus,
you'll start in verdant Panther Meadows, which is often awash in floral
splendor.

Take the Central Mount Shasta exit off I-5 and go east 0.7 mile on
Lake Street. Curve left onto Everitt Memorial Highway and continue
13.5 miles to the parking area for Panther Meadows Campground on
the right.

Read the flyers near the trailhead about the ecology of Panther
Meadows and the resultant need to stay on the designated trail when
passing through, then take the path from the parking lot's east side.
Quickly reach a trail fork and continue straight (hike 51 goes to the
left). Slowly saunter through Panther Meadows and admire the osten-
tatious display of red paintbrush and the more subtle attractions of
yellow monkey-flowers and pink-flowered meadow heather.

Leave the meadow behind at 0.2 mile, pass the self-issue permit station for day hikers, and climb through a red fir and mountain hemlock
forest that features copious quantities of mint-scented pennyroyal. A
trail fork awaits at 0.6 mile. Hike 50 heads left, but bear right to walk
nearly level along Gray Butte's north ridge, a vantage point that offers
tantalizing, tree-filtered views of Red Butte to the east and other
mountains to the west.

Descend briefly to the east side of the ridge, then angle up the steep
slope past vast stretches of talus boulders. Enjoy views of Mount
Shasta and other regions and peaks, then swing westerly at a switchback at 1.2 miles. Continue a gentle ascent to reach a saddle at 1.5
miles. An obvious trail runs south 150 yards to radio towers, but follow
a faint, intermittent path northeast up the open ridge another 0.2 mile

A cloud-enshrouded Mount Shasta looms large above the summit of Gray Butte.

to the top of Gray Butte, which provides a home for much pinemat manzanita, a bit of bush chinquapin, several red firs and mountain hemlocks, and one prostrate whitebark pine.

Find a flat rock and enjoy the vast panorama. From this vantage point, you can observe mountains in all of northern California's geological provinces. The Cascade Range includes Mount Shasta and stretches southeast down to Lassen Peak and its entourage in and around Lassen Park. Farther south, the Sierra Nevada begins its long journey to Lake Tahoe and Yosemite. Far to the east is the Modoc Plateau, while even farther to the east, the Basin and Range province stretches into Nevada. Look for the Sacramento Valley to the south, with the Coast Range rising to its west. To your west are the vast array of granitic and metamorphic mountains of the Klamaths, epitomized by Castle Crags and the Mount Eddy range.

Other prominent features lie near Gray Butte: Look south to see McCloud; to the west, you'll spy Black Butte, the southern section of the town of Mount Shasta, and the enticing blue of Lake Siskiyou.

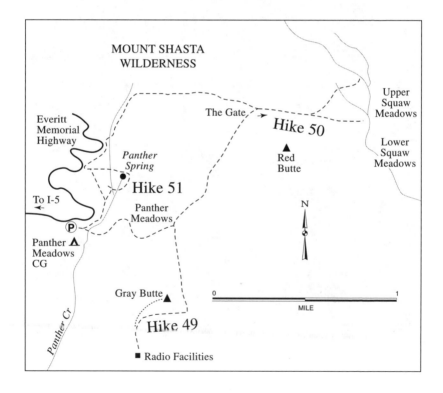

50 SQUAW MEADOWS

Length: 5.2 miles round trip
Hiking time: 3 hours
High point: 7,900 feet
Total elevation gain: 1,100 feet
Difficulty: moderate
Season: early July through mid-October
Water: bring your own
Maps: USGS 7.5' McCloud, USFS Mt. Shasta Wilderness
Permit: required; available just beyond Panther Meadows for day hikes; obtain from Mount Shasta Ranger District or McCloud Ranger District for overnight trips; dogs prohibited
Nearest campground: Panther Meadows Campground
Information: Mount Shasta Ranger District; Shasta-Trinity National Forest

Map on page 132

This hike is for adventurous souls who don't mind when the trail occasionally fades and they have to scramble over rocks, trek across a snowfield, or descend through an open forest. But the rewards are ample: beautiful wildflowers, close-up views of Mount Shasta, proximity to the steep flanks of Red Butte, and the lush greenery of secluded Squaw Meadows.

Take the Central Mount Shasta exit off I-5 and go east 0.7 mile on Lake Street. Swing left onto Everitt Memorial Highway, then climb 13.5 miles and park on the right at Panther Meadows Campground.

Before starting the hike, take the time to read the flyers at the trailhead. They discuss the necessity of protecting the sensitive plants of Panther Meadows and Squaw Meadows. Always stay on designated paths and minimize damage to the ecosystem by stepping only on rocks, bare soil, and snow.

Head east to a trail fork at 0.1 mile. Hike 51 goes north to explore the upper reaches of Panther Meadows, but head straight, enjoying a gorgeous vista of Mount Shasta and passing three small streams that help provide moisture for the flowers, grasses, and meadow heather of lower Panther Meadows. Reach the end of the meadow and the self-issue permit station at 0.2 mile, then start a stiff climb past profuse quantities of pennyroyal (check for the smell of mint) and the comforting presence of red firs and mountain hemlocks.

Reach a trail fork at 0.6 mile. Hike 49 goes right, but go left, soon reaching a saddle. From there, descend towards the looming presence of Red Butte to reach a gully and the Mount Shasta Wilderness boundary at 0.8 mile. Follow rock ducks up and over a small ridge, then regain good trail and climb steeply, noting that a few whitebark pines have joined the forest. The forest soon parts, giving southeasterly vistas of McCloud, the large meadows surrounding Squaw Valley Creek south of McCloud, and the distant face of Lassen Peak and other Lassen Park notables. You'll also have the first good view of Mount Shasta since leaving Panther Meadows.

Begin a brief descent at 1.2 miles that leads to an open field of sand and wildflowers where the trail essentially disappears. Follow near the boulders at the base of Red Butte for 0.2 mile, regain obvious trail, then go right at a trail fork at 1.5 miles (a left leads 1.1 miles to the old Ski Bowl and beyond to hike 51).

A small saddle holding whitebark pines and a lone red fir awaits at 1.6 miles. Descend east through The Gate and enjoy views of distant mountains. Drop down gently, then reach a trail fork at 1.9 miles. The 0.4-mile trail to the left drops, contours awhile, then rises to upper Squaw Meadows, home to lush grasses and an excellent view of Mount Shasta ridges. The occasionally faint 0.4-mile trail to the right drops down through the forest to the northwest edge of lower Squaw Meadows. Walk above the north edge for 200 yards to a stream flowing in on the northeast side. Once there, you'll see Red Butte standing guard over the verdant greenery; the pink flowers of meadow heather and the white spikes of corn lily accent the meadow's lushness.

51 PANTHER MEADOWS

Length: 1.3 miles round trip
Hiking time: 1 hour, day hike only
High point: 7,750 feet
Total elevation gain: 350 feet
Difficulty: easy
Season: late June through October
Water: bring your own
Maps: USGS 7.5' McCloud, USFS Mt. Shasta Wilderness
Permit: none required
Nearest campground: Panther Meadows Campground
Information: Mount Shasta Ranger District, Shasta-Trinity National Forest

Map on page 132

This short walk takes you through Panther Meadows, an area of magnificent beauty that is sacred to many Native Americans. You'll visit Panther Springs, see wildflowers, have awe-inspiring views of Mount Shasta, and be able to gaze far south to distant mountains. Note that swimming and wading is prohibited and that there can be no more than ten people in a group.

From I-5, take the Central Mount Shasta exit. Go east 0.7 mile on Lake Street, then curve left onto Everitt Memorial Highway. Travel 13.5 miles and turn right into the parking area for Panther Meadows Campground.

Before starting the hike, put yourself in a proper frame of mind. You're entering a site that is not only of great spiritual importance but which also contains a very delicate ecosystem. Subalpine meadows such as Panther Meadows (and hike 50's Squaw Meadows) are rare on Mount Shasta because the porous volcanic soil doesn't retain water near the surface. However, springs feed Panther Meadows, making the association of grasses, annual flowers, and meadow heather possible. Meadow heather can take 400 years to grow to a height of 8 inches, and one careless step can set it back 200 years. So please stay on the designated trail and make sure your steps land on bare ground, rocks, or snow.

Read the informational leaflets at the trailhead, then find the hike's beginning on the east side of the parking area. Walk past a campsite and continue 100 yards to a trail fork at the western edge of Panther Meadows. Hikes 49 and 50 continue straight to Gray Butte and Squaw

Panther Meadows

Meadows. Your route goes left and up along the meadow. Numerous signs direct you away from sensitive areas and keep you on the proper path, where you'll have opportunities to observe red paintbrush, yellow monkey-flower, and the pink blossoms of meadow heather.

Approach Panther Creek at 0.2 mile, then climb steeply away and into a forest of red fir and mountain hemlock with the sound of the tumbling brook in your ears. The forest soon thins to reveal the majesty of Mount Shasta's southern flanks. See Sargent's Ridge climbing east of the old Ski Bowl to meet Shastarama Point and then Thumb Rock and the mountain's airy summit.

Reach another trail fork at 0.5 mile. Go right and then right again before crossing the creek. Continue upward through the verdant meadow to quickly reach Panther Spring, a sacred site for many Native Americans. Show proper respect by preventing any pollution or erosion.

The way soon leads to another spring. Beyond, the path briefly dips, then rises to allow a southward vista of the Sacramento River drainage, the distant Sacramento Valley, and the Coast Range southwest of Redding. Bear left at 0.7 mile (a right quickly brings you to the Everitt Memorial Highway and a parking area), then go right 0.1 mile farther to rejoin previously walked trail for the downhill stroll to the trailhead.

Nearby: Two other hiking options begin from the old Ski Bowl parking area, which is another 0.6 mile up Everitt Memorial Highway from Panther Meadows Campground. One hike leaves from a large open space on the right (look for barricading boulders and several picnic tables) and heads northeast to meet the Squaw Meadows trail (hike 50) just west of The Gate. The other travels past the remnants of the Ski Bowl (badly damaged in a 1978 avalanche) and up the slopes of Mount Shasta.

52 MOUNT SHASTA SUMMIT VIA AVALANCHE GULCH

Length: 12 miles round trip
Hiking time: 9 hours or 2 days
High point: 14,162 feet
Total elevation gain: 7,300 feet
Difficulty: very strenuous
Season: early May to late September
Water: none reliably available beyond Horse Camp except for snow
Maps: USGS 7.5' McCloud, USGS 7.5' Mt. Shasta, USFS Mt. Shasta Wilderness
Permit: required; available at the trailhead for day hikes; obtain from Mount Shasta Ranger District or McCloud Ranger District for overnight trips; dogs prohibited
Nearest campground: McBride Springs Campground
Information: Mount Shasta Ranger District, Shasta-Trinity National Forest

Eternally clad in white, Mount Shasta towers 10,000 feet above surrounding terrain to dominate northern California. This massive and imposing volcano, a bulwark of the Cascade Range that stretches from Lassen Peak to southern British Columbia, attracts people from around the world. Some are drawn to the spiritual power of the mountain and are content to worship from below; others see Shasta and know they want to experience the ultimate energy high obtainable only at the summit.

This hike takes you up the least-difficult route to the power pinnacle. But be forewarned that achieving the 14,162-foot goal involves careful planning, having the proper equipment and supplies, and being in good physical condition. Bring good boots, crampons, an ice ax, plenty of warm clothes, a tent or other form of shelter, lots of food and water, a stove for melting snow for drinking water, a wide-brimmed hat, good sunglasses, strong sunblock, and a good topographical map. Be prepared for sudden storms and always check the weather forecast before beginning. (The Fifth Season, an outdoor-equipment store, has a 24-hour mountain conditions number for climbers and skiers, 916-926-5555.) If the weather turns nasty while you're climbing, turn around and hustle back to the trailhead. And note that you'll be climbing primarily on snow, especially early in the season, so get an early start—the first hint of dawn is not too early—so that your crampons will get excellent traction in the hard snow and ice. Finally, use bags provided at the trailhead and at the Mount Shasta Ranger District to pack out feces (read the directions).

To begin the adventure, take the Central Mount Shasta exit off I-5 and, if you're doing an overnight trip, stop by the Mount Shasta Ranger District at 204 West Alma for a permit and bag. Go east 0.7 mile on Lake Street. Bend left onto the Everitt Memorial Highway and travel 11 miles to Bunny Flat.

Start the ascent along the west side of a dry meadow, then enter a red fir forest. The trail from Sand Flat comes in from the left at 1.2 miles, and the Sierra Club cabin (off-limits except in emergencies) and meadow of Horse Camp appear at 1.8 miles. Horse Camp makes a great camping spot (and final destination for day hikers): There is an excellent source of water, a solar-composting toilet, a knowledgeable

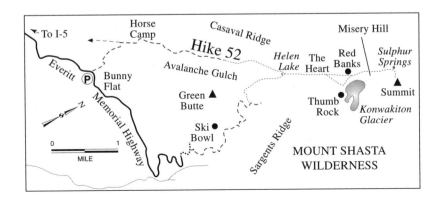

The view from Bunny Flat of Avalanche Gulch, the most popular route to Mount Shasta's summit (Photo by Noelle Parnell Soares)

Sierra Club caretaker, and a great view of what lies ahead. Campers must pay a fee to the caretaker.

Continue the climb up Olberman's Causeway, a series of flat stones. When it ends near the tree line, you'll follow faint trails northwest until you reach snow and put on your crampons. The way soon reaches the west side of Avalanche Gulch and rises at 4 miles to Helen Lake, elevation 10,443 feet. In most years, Helen Lake is no more than a flat snowfield, but it does serve as a good first-day destination for those doing the climb in 2 days.

The real grind begins above Helen Lake as you make your way up Avalanche Gulch. Be on the lookout for falling rocks as the route steepens and you approach The Heart, a bare patch near 12,000 feet. Go right and head for the gap between Thumb Rock and the Red Banks. From here, continue up, with Konwakiton Glacier on your right and the Red Banks on your left. If this seems too dangerous, drop back the way you came and climb up through one of the steep chutes in the Red Banks.

Above the Red Banks, Misery Hill awaits those who've survived thus far; it begins at 13,000 feet and rises 800 feet to a relatively flat area. From here, you're home free. Continue north and pass just east of Sulphur Springs, which helped keep John Muir from freezing to death. Head briefly east and make the final, short scramble to Mount Shasta's summit, the object of your desire for hours, days, or decades.

Breathe in the thin, clean air as you revel in your accomplishment and survey the panorama you worked so hard to win. What a panorama it is: The Cascades stretch north to far haze in Oregon and south to

Lassen Peak, where they disappear under the northern realm of the mighty Sierra Nevada; forested mountains march south to the Sacramento Valley and the Coast Range; rocky spires and broad-shouldered ridges of the Klamaths stretch to the west, with the Pacific Ocean a distant gleam on exceptionally clear days; to the northeast and east, you'll see the high desert of northern California merging with those of southern Oregon and northwestern Nevada.

Note that there is an alternate route to Helen Lake which leaves from the old Ski Bowl at the end of Everitt Memorial Highway, 2.5 miles beyond Bunny Flat. It begins at 7,800 feet, 900 or so feet higher than Bunny Flat. Follow it up 2 miles to about the 9,600-foot level, cut cross-country over to Green Butte ridge, then make your way to Helen Lake. Everitt Memorial Highway is not plowed, so you have to wait until all the snow melts on the road. This often doesn't happen until early July, when you'll have the disadvantage of walking on the loose dirt and talus of the Ski Bowl. This alternate route is best if you hike late in the season, when there's no snow on the mountain below the elevation of Helen Lake. It also makes an excellent day-hike option any time the road's open.

53 WHITNEY FALLS

Length: 3.6 miles round trip
Hiking time: 2 hours or 2 days
High point: 6,250 feet
Total elevation gain: 800 feet
Difficulty: moderate
Season: mid-June through mid-October
Water: bring your own
Maps: USGS 7.5' Mt. Shasta, USFS Mt. Shasta Wilderness
Permit: required; available at the trailhead for day hikes; obtain from Mount Shasta Ranger District or McCloud Ranger District for overnight trips; dogs prohibited
Nearest campground: McBride Springs Campground
Information: Mount Shasta Ranger District, Shasta-Trinity National Forest

This walk on the north slopes of Mount Shasta takes you to the edge of the deep valley holding Whitney Creek and Whitney Falls, a magical mixture of mountain and water. You'll also have intimate views of Mount Shasta and Shastina, in addition to a wide-ranging panorama to the west and north. Camping opportunities are limited, although determined individuals can find an occasional level spot. Note that the flow of Whitney Creek can vary from a trickle to a torrent. It's at its highest during storms and hot, late-summer days.

Take the Highway 97 exit off I-5 in Weed, travel 0.7 mile, then take 97 northeast from the flashing light. Travel 8 miles, then turn right onto an unsigned dirt road. (If you reach Road A12, you've gone 0.3

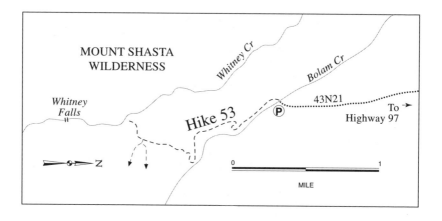

mile too far.) This bumpy dirt road, 43N21, takes you all the way to the trailhead. Bear right at 0.3 mile and at 1.1 miles, cross railroad tracks (look first!) at 1.7 miles, go right at 2.1 miles and 2.4 miles, then reach the trailhead at 4.1 miles.

Note the informative signboard and the day-hike wilderness permit station, then head right to a crossing of Bolam Creek and the first views of Mount Shasta and partner Shastina looming large to the south. Look for Whitney Glacier pushing down through the valley separating the two volcanoes, with Bolam Glacier a mile to the east.

The path, an old dirt road, quickly turns southeasterly, traveling through an area populated by Jeffrey pine, white fir, greenleaf manzanita, antelopebrush, rabbitbrush, and mountain mahogany; the latter three are common members of desert plant communities. At 0.6 mile,

The self-issue day-hike permit station at the trailhead for Whitney Falls

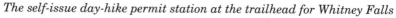

the trail curves briefly west, giving a vista of hilly Shasta Valley; beyond, the endless peaks and ridges of the Klamath Mountains range west toward the coast and north into Oregon.

Continue upward and southward, then turn right off the dirt road at 1.6 miles onto a narrow path marked by a rock duck. Climb and then run level through a forest of Jeffrey pines and red and white firs that allows some light for currants to grow.

Join several large Jeffrey pines at the rim of Whitney Creek's U-shaped valley at 1.8 miles. Here the sweep and scope of life and landscape will fill your body and spirit with uplifting energy. From on high, Mount Shasta, Shastina, and Whitney Glacier exude natural power. Just up the valley, Whitney Creek leaps down 200 feet to crash on rocks below. A basalt lava flow has dropped talus onto the valley's west rim, providing a stark foreground for Mount Eddy and environs looming beyond.

The edge of the canyon is a great place to have a picnic and watch birds fly through the open space. Bring a tarp and lie on your back to watch the everchanging shapes of clouds that form above Shasta's high reaches.

54 BREWER CREEK

Length: 3.8 miles round trip
Hiking time: 3 hours or overnight
High point: 7,850 feet
Total elevation gain: 500 feet
Difficulty: easy to moderate
Season: early July through mid-October
Water: bring your own
Maps: USGS 7.5' Mt. Shasta, USFS Mt. Shasta Wilderness
Permit: required; available at the trailhead for day hikes; obtain from Mount Shasta Ranger District or McCloud Ranger District for overnight trips; dogs prohibited
Nearest campground: Fowlers Camp Campground
Information: Mount Shasta Ranger District, Shasta-Trinity National Forest

This gentle hike offers an easy way to explore the seldom-visited east flanks of Mount Shasta. Walk near the tree line, where you'll be tantalized by views of Shasta's massive glaciers and lofty summit. Note that camping is allowed on the mountain (follow regulations posted at the trailhead), but this hike is best done in one day. Some good advice: Buy the USFS Mount Shasta Wilderness topographical map; it will guide you through the maze of roads leading to the trailhead, show you the trail, and help you identify major Mount Shasta landmarks.

Take the Highway 97 exit off I-5 in Weed, travel 0.7 mile, then take

A view of stunted whitebark pines and the east flank of Mount Shasta from near Brewer Creek

97 northeast from the flashing light. Travel 15 miles, turn right onto Road 19 (look for the Deer Mountain Road sign), and go 19 miles to the Brewer Creek Trailhead sign and a junction with Road 42N02. Alternatively, reach this junction by driving Highway 89 for 3 miles east of McCloud, turning left onto Pilgrim Creek Road, driving 7 miles, then turning left onto Road 19 and traveling 15 miles. Take 42N02, bearing left at a major road fork at 2 miles. Turn left 0.8 mile farther onto Road 42N10 and follow it through junctions with lesser roads for 3 miles to the trailhead.

Make your first order of business a visit to the signboard and self-issue permit station. Then, armed with a permit and pertinent information about safety and Mount Shasta's natural history, take the first step onto the trail. Numerous red firs, from little babies to mature 100-footers, form most of the forest, with the occasional addition of a western white pine. You'll see a few stumps as you continue, evidence of past logging.

Climb moderately and pass the wilderness boundary at 0.2 mile; then meet the first switchback at 0.4 mile. Climb west on more switchbacks,

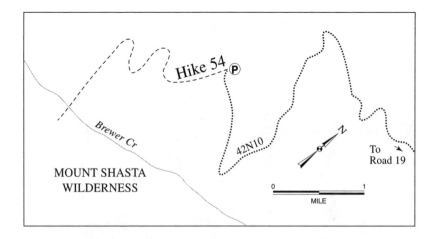

eventually reaching an elevation comfortable for whitebark pines but not for western whites.

Most of the serious climbing is out of the way by 1.3 miles, where you begin a southern run past blue lupines, red paintbrush, white and purple phlox, and other flowers. You'll soon reach an open area with the hike's first good views. Look west up the slopes of mighty Shasta at Wintun and Hotlum glaciers, then farther up to the summit that towers 6,500 feet above you. The eastern vista contains Ash Creek Butte and several other nearby volcanoes, with forested ridges stretching into the distance.

Cross Brewer Creek at 1.7 miles, then follow the trail another 0.2 mile to its end near a small ridge. For more hiking, follow an old jeep road west up the mountain or continue southeast for 200 yards up and over the ridge to gain views through whitebark pines of Lassen Peak.

The Lower Falls of the McCloud River is a popular recreation spot.

55 LOWER AND MIDDLE FALLS OF THE MCCLOUD RIVER

Length: 2.4 miles round trip
Hiking time: 2 hours
High point: 3,350 feet
Total elevation gain: 300 feet
Difficulty: easy
Season: year-round; some winter snow
Water: available from the McCloud River; purify first
Map: USGS 7.5' Lake McCloud
Permit: none required
Nearest campground: Fowlers Camp Campground
Information: McCloud Ranger District, Shasta-Trinity National Forest

Born of the glacial ice and alpine snows that gild Mount Shasta, the frigid waters of the McCloud River surge swiftly south to merge with the Pit and Sacramento rivers at Shasta Lake. This hike travels the banks of this majestic river, reaching two magnificent waterfalls that pour forth invigorating energy that will suffuse every cell in your body.

Take Highway 89 for 15 miles east of the junction of 89 and I-5, and 5 miles east of McCloud, then turn south onto a dirt road signed for national forest river access and wildlife viewing. Go 0.6 mile, stay straight at a road fork, bear right 50 yards farther, then continue another 0.7 mile past Fowlers Camp Campground to the trailhead at the Lower Falls of the McCloud River picnic area.

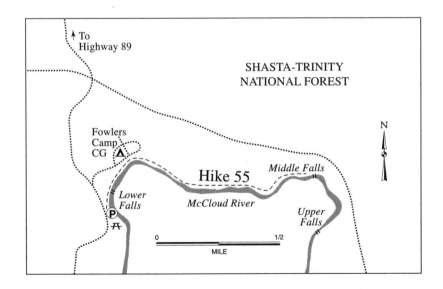

The Middle Falls of the McCloud River

Let the sound of crashing water draw you to a wooden bench and railing with a prime view of the Lower Falls. Walk down the wooden steps and then cross over rocks to the edge of the McCloud River, where you'll see the 10-foot cascade plunging into a deep pool.

Take the paved path when you're ready to continue upstream to the even more impressive Middle Falls. Note the trailside talus basalt jumbles and those on the south bank of the river as the way leads along the southeast edge of Fowlers Camp Campground (accessed by several side trails) and to another wooden bench and a sign detailing the region's human history.

Reach a Middle Falls Trail sign and a trail tread change to dirt at 0.4 mile. You now travel a gentle, riverside path that's shaded by Douglas firs, with occasional help from dogwoods and other trees.

Gain the first invigorating glimpse of the Middle Falls at 1 mile, then hurry the last 0.2 mile to reach the stupendous cascade. Seventy feet wide and 35 feet high, the waterfall is split by a huge buttress and an intervening ledge before it bursts with a cacophonous roar into a seafoam-green pool, simultaneously spawning sheets of swirling mist that drift downstream toward a steep cliff spiked with surreal hoodoos.

Topped with towering ponderosa pines, more cliffs guard the large pool at the falls' base. The sparsely vegetated cliff on the north side receives much exposure to the sun; the southern cliff sees little direct sunlight and consequently harbors a lush green undergrowth of ferns and other plants. Good swimmers with a high tolerance for cold water can scramble over the basalt boulders to the pool's edge for a brief immersion that will increase sensory awareness by several orders of magnitude.

Nearby: To visit yet another waterfall, head for Hedge Creek Falls. Find the trailhead on the west side of I-5's Dunsmuir Avenue/Siskiyou Avenue exit, which is 5 miles south of the intersection of I-5 and Highway 89. Begin at the gazebo, which offers a full view of Mount Shasta. The 200-yard path switchbacks down under Douglas fir shade to the serene beauty of the falls, which tumble an unimpeded 20 feet from a rock lip. The main attraction is immediately behind the falls: a large cave 60 feet wide, 20 feet deep, and 10 feet high. Within its cool recesses, water drips from small springs and leached minerals have stained the walls rust and yellow.

56 MCCLOUD RIVER PRESERVE

Length: 5.4 miles round trip
Hiking time: 4 hours, day hike only
High point: 2,100 feet
Total elevation gain: 350 feet
Difficulty: easy to moderate
Season: early April through November
Water: available from the McCloud River; purify first
Maps: USGS 7.5' Shoeinhorse Mtn, USGS 7.5' Yellowjacket Mtn
Permit: none required
Nearest campground: Ah-Di-Na Campground
Information: The Nature Conservancy's McCloud River Preserve

The McCloud River Preserve encompasses a lush area of diverse flora that grows above and beside one of the most beautiful stretches of mountain river in the world. The trail travels past dense stands of verdant growth reminiscent of tropical rain forests, through open tracts of pine/fir forest frequented by gray squirrels and Steller's jays, and along the tumbling, blue-gray waters of the river itself, where numerous swimming holes offer icy refreshment on hot summer days and steep, tree-clad slopes stretch 2,000 feet into the sky.

Reach the McCloud River Preserve by traveling Highway 89 to McCloud, then turning south onto Squaw Creek Road. Travel 9 miles to McCloud Reservoir, then stay above the lake's west shore. Reach a fork that is 11.4 miles from Highway 89, where you turn right onto Road 38N53, an occasionally bumpy (though easily two-wheel-drive passable) dirt road. Following signs for Ah-Di-Na Campground and

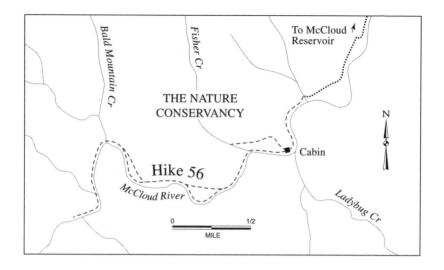

The Nature Conservancy, stay left at a road fork at 12 miles, go straight at another fork at 13.8 miles, continue past Ah-Di-Na Campground at 17.4 miles, then reach the parking area at 18.5 miles.

Cross a small stream on a wooden bridge to a sign that gives important information about the McCloud River Preserve (pets, camping, and removing anything are prohibited). For those interested in fly fishing for rainbow and German brown trout, note that it is catch-and-release with single, barbless hooks and artificial lures. Here at the McCloud River Preserve, The Nature Conservancy protects the natural attributes of the McCloud River and its canyon, conducts scientific studies, and educates visitors about the importance of protecting the environment.

Start down towards the river past Douglas fir, ponderosa pine, bigleaf maple, and dogwood, common tree species that are joined later by white fir, sugar pine, incense cedar, black oak, canyon live oak, Pacific yew, and white alder. Soon you'll reach the edge of the mighty McCloud, where the path leads downstream. Note the metamorphic rocks underfoot. You're walking near the eastern edge of the Klamath Mountains; farther east and north you'd find only basalt and other types of volcanic rock common to the Cascades.

The caretaker cabin awaits at 0.4 mile. Here you sign in and gather a trail map, a guide to the nature trail, and information about The Nature Conservancy. Note that a side trail leaves from here and travels 0.3 mile north to a small set of waterfalls on Fisher Creek (best in April and May). Just beyond the cabin is the first of 18 numbered posts keyed to the guide to the nature trail; follow the short path for an introduction to local human and natural history that includes identification of a large variety of plant species.

Continue in the downstream direction, alternating between succulent stretches of greenery and more open areas near the river. Reach a

The McCloud River Preserve trail has many vantage points for observing the river's tumbling waters. (Photo by Noelle Parnell Soares)

trail fork at 0.8 mile; a left takes you by the river, past a yew tree grove, and then to a swimming spot, the first of many. The upper portion of the trail rejoins at 1.3 miles.

The trail briefly splits again at 1.6 miles, then continues to cross Bald Mountain Creek at 2 miles. The way now heads south past more spectacular scenery, eventually ending at 2.7 miles near a rope that spans the river.

57 SQUAW VALLEY CREEK

Length: 8.2 miles round trip
Hiking time: 5 hours or 2 days
High point: 2,500 feet
Total elevation gain: 500 feet
Difficulty: easy
Season: mid-April through November; other times when weather and road conditions allow
Water: available from Squaw Valley Creek; purify first
Maps: USGS 7.5' Girard Ridge, USGS 7.5' Yellowjacket Mtn
Permit: none required
Nearest campground: Fowlers Camp Campground
Information: McCloud Ranger District, Shasta-Trinity National Forest

Squaw Valley Creek's waterfalls and cascades demand most of your attention on this hike, but occasionally let your eyes rise up the deep

Numerous tiger lilies grow near the banks of Squaw Valley Creek.

green of the steep, forested mountainsides that guide the stream down to its merging with the McCloud River. This gently sloping trail along the creek's west side makes an excellent day hike or an easy spring warm-up for more strenuous summer backpacking treks.

To reach the trailhead, take Highway 89 to McCloud and go south on Squaw Valley Road. After 5.9 miles, turn right onto a dirt road that's signed for Squaw Valley Creek and the Pacific Crest Trail. Travel a smooth 3 miles, cross Squaw Valley Creek on a concrete bridge, then park in the lot on the left.

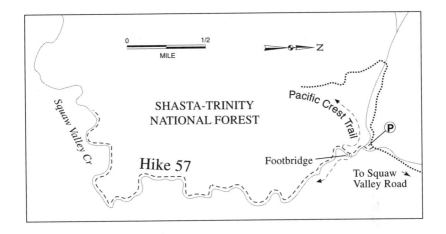

Take the dirt road downstream to a wooden bridge across a tributary, then continue on the path through a forest dominated by Douglas fir, with lesser quantities of dogwood and vine maple and an occasional guest appearance by ponderosa pine, incense cedar, and Pacific yew. Near Squaw Valley Creek, look for willow, alder, and an abundance of the huge leaves of the umbrella plant.

Quickly reach a meeting with the Pacific Crest Trail. Walk to the middle of the PCT bridge for a bird's-eye view of Squaw Valley Creek tumbling through a narrow gorge. Just downstream of the bridge is an excellent swimming hole, one of a dozen or so scattered along the route (look for side trails). If you do swim, be aware that the water is very cold: Make sure that you can get out quickly and safely.

Walk briefly uphill and downstream along the PCT, then part company when it heads farther up to the right at 0.4 mile. As you descend gently, look to the east for a view of a fire-scarred ridge punctuated with stark tree skeletons. Pass through a grove of Pacific yew at 0.9 mile, then reach the creekside and dozens of tiger lilies and thousands of horsetails.

Climb well above the creek, then drop down to a level area at 2 miles that has one good campsite and several other potential sites. Just beyond, a side trail leads to an 8-foot waterfall, which is followed in quick succession by another waterfall, and then a series of cascades. Guarded by large canyon live oaks, the most impressive cataract awaits at 2.8 miles: On one side it surges 15 feet through a chute; on the other it drops down a two-tiered embankment.

Farther along, pass two more waterfalls and an outcropping of metamorphic rock, then note increased amounts of poison oak. At 4 miles, pass through a small saddle and a sunny grove of young black oaks, then note a side trail down to another good campsite.

The main trail soon fades out on the steep mountainside. Plans call for extending the trail another mile to a dirt road near Bear Trap Creek. Call the McCloud Ranger District for more information.

58   INDIAN CREEK AND FLUME TRAILS

Length: 2.6 miles round trip
Hiking time: 2 hours, day hike only
High point: 2,200 feet
Total elevation gain: 300 feet
Difficulty: easy
Season: year-round; occasional winter snow
Water: available from Indian Creek; purify first
Maps: USGS 7.5' Dunsmuir, USFS Castle Crags Wilderness
Permit: none required
Nearest campground: Castle Crags State Park Campground
Information: Castle Crags State Park

Both natural and human history highlight this hike's trails. The Indian Creek Trail features 29 numbered posts that help you identify twenty-one different trees and shrubs; you'll also learn about human exploitation of the area's timber and minerals (buy the interpretive booklet at park headquarters). The Flume Trail travels through shaded forest and visits human artifacts, an old wooden flume among them.

Drive 6 miles south of Dunsmuir or 48 miles north of Redding on I-5, then take the Castle Crags State Park/Castella exit. Following signs for the park, go west 0.3 mile, then turn right. Park to the left just beyond park headquarters.

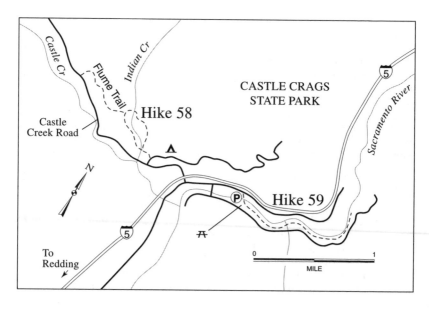

The steep granite slabs of Castle Crags rise high above the Indian Creek Trail.

Begin on the Indian Creek Trail. Bear left at a trail fork at 0.1 mile and start a gentle ascent. You'll soon cross Indian Creek, which has its source at Indian Springs just south of Castle Dome. Shortly afterward, the canopy opens to reveal northwesterly views of the granite spires of Castle Crags, some of which stretch to heights of 6,500 feet.

At 0.5 mile, turn left on the Flume Trail. This 0.8-mile path soon parallels an elevated wooden flume that was part of an old system that brought some of Castle Creek's water to Castella. The trail continues through a ponderosa pine and Douglas fir forest, crosses a footbridge over a small creek, then descends to some environmental campsites near Castle Creek Road.

When you're ready, return the way you came to the Indian Creek Trail. Head left and uphill to another crossing of Indian Creek, then do the downhill roll to the trailhead. Note that another interpretive nature trail, much shorter than the Indian Creek Trail, leaves from just behind park headquarters.

59 RIVER TRAIL

Length: 2.2 miles round trip
Hiking time: 2 hours, day hike only
High point: 2,100 feet
Total elevation gain: 100 feet
Difficulty: easy
Season: year-round; occasional winter snow
Water: bring your own
Maps: USGS 7.5' Dunsmuir, USFS Castle Crags Wilderness
Permit: none required
Nearest campground: Castle Crags State Park Campground
Information: Castle Crags State Park

Map on page 152

The Sacramento River is born as snowmelt on the slopes of Mount Shasta and other peaks. It starts small, gathering the waters of numerous tributaries and springs near its headwaters, and then grows as it accepts the large flows of the McCloud and Pit rivers in what is now Shasta Lake. Farther south, Cottonwood Creek, Mill Creek, Deer Creek, and other streams flow from the Cascades, Coast Range, and Northern Sierra to pump up the mighty waterway, which eventually merges with the vast Pacific Ocean near San Francisco. This easy walk takes you along the banks of the fledgling Sacramento, where it is still surrounded by its smaller sources in the airy mountain realm.

Take the I-5 Castle Crags State Park/Castella exit, which is 6 miles south of Dunsmuir and 48 miles north of Redding. Go east, then turn left onto Frontage Road. Travel 0.5 mile north, then note the wide shoulder on the right next to several picnic tables. Continue to the northern end of the shoulder and park near the River Trail sign.

Head down some steps, cross under the railroad tracks, then walk past a water fountain. Reach a footbridge across the Sacramento River and pause in the middle to watch the water flow by. In the summer of 1991, a railroad accident just to the north dumped a toxic compound into the river that killed every living thing downstream all the way to Shasta Lake. The fish population is making a comeback, as are many other plants and animals. As you explore, look for signs of life in the waters.

The trail continues upstream along the east bank. For the first half mile, you'll travel well above the water, though several steep side trails let you reach the river. To the west, you can look out over the tops of water-loving willows and alders to the granite cathedrals of Castle Crags. To the east, you'll see a mixed forest of ponderosa pine, Douglas fir, incense cedar, and black oak stretching up the slope.

The path eventually takes you along the river banks and runs fairly level for the last stretch. If you desire swimming on the way back to the trailhead, you'll find a few spots where the stream flow slows.

Young rafters ride the riffles on the Sacramento River in Castle Crags State Park.

60 INDIAN SPRINGS AND CASTLE DOME

Length: 5.4 miles round trip
Hiking time: 4 hours, day hike only
High point: 4,800 feet
Total elevation gain: 2,200 feet
Difficulty: strenuous
Season: early April through mid-November
Water: none except at Indian Springs; purify first; bring plenty
Maps: USGS 7.5' Dunsmuir, USFS Castle Crags Wilderness
Permit: none required
Nearest campground: Castle Crags State Park Campground
Information: Castle Crags State Park

From I-5, Castle Crags is an unexpected sight, its cliffs and hillocks of granite riding high above and isolated from the surrounding forested ridges. The steep trail to Castle Dome allows you to visit the eastern edge of this geological realm, where you can investigate firsthand the stone shapes left by glacial action and millions of years of erosional processes. Another reward is the sweeping view of Mount Shasta and other northern California peaks.

Take the I-5 Castle Crags State Park/Castella exit, which is 48 miles north of Redding and 6 miles south of Dunsmuir. Go west and follow signs to the park. Turn right just past park headquarters (where you'll

Castle Dome looms high above a hiker on the Castle Dome Trail.

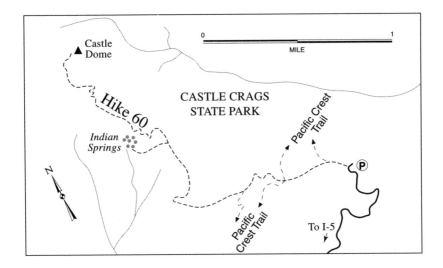

pay an entrance fee and obtain brochures). Head 0.3 mile through the campground, then climb a curvy mile to the vista point.

Head back down the road 150 feet from the vista point parking area to find the trail's beginning. Level tread brings you to a trail fork at 0.2 mile. Go left and continue walking in the shade of Douglas firs, white firs, ponderosa pines, and incense cedars. These large conifers, along with the occasional grove of black oaks, shelter you for most of the ascent.

Join the Pacific Crest Trail at 0.5 mile for a brief jaunt, then go right at the next trail fork, and then right again at yet another trail fork at 1 mile. Continue ever upward, letting your burning thighs set a vigorous rhythm for your heart and lungs.

At 2 miles, a side trail to the left presents a welcome diversion. Follow it 400 yards to the verdant dampness of Indian Springs, where water trickles from cracks in a rock face in the shade of bigleaf maples, dogwoods, and incense cedars. Note that Indian Springs is the hike's only sure source of water.

Above the Indian Springs turnoff, the main trail soon rises above the forest and among the angled granite pinnacles and slabs, where you'll have increasingly spectacular views, near and far.

The trail ends at 2.7 miles near a cable fence. The bald visage of massive Castle Dome looms to the right, while the rest of the Crags shoot skyward to the left. Mount Shasta, the undisputed mountain king of northern California, looms large to the northeast. Forests clothe the ranges of mountains stretching east beyond the Sacramento River. To the south, Grey Rocks punctuate Flume Ridge just beyond the Castle Creek Valley, with Shasta Bally and Bully Choop farther south.

You may see people climbing to the top of Castle Dome. If you wish to do the same, you must have solid expertise in rock climbing, shoes with good tread, and dry rock for those shoes to get good traction. The route with the least amount of danger starts on the dome's south side, then follows a crack up along the east side. Watch your footing and re-member that climbing up is usually easier than climbing down.

Nearby: For those desiring more hiking, the Root Creek trail makes a nice 1.5-mile addition to the day's walk. Return to the PCT (four cor-ners) trail fork encountered on the way up and go left. Stay to your left at two trail forks, following signs toward Root Creek. The way then runs level under Douglas firs and ponderosa pines to the banks of Root Creek. Sit on one of the benches surrounded by incense cedars, white alders, and vine maples as you listen to the clear water spill over a se-ries of 3-foot waterfalls.

61 SULPHUR CREEK AND BURSTARSE FALLS

Length: 6.4 miles round trip
Hiking time: 4 hours
High point: 3,250 feet
Total elevation gain: 950 feet
Difficulty: moderate
Season: year-round; some winter snow
Water: available from creeks; purify first
Maps: USGS 7.5' Dunsmuir, USFS Castle Crags Wilderness
Permit: none required
Nearest campground: Castle Crags State Park Campground
Information: Mount Shasta Ranger District, Shasta-Trinity National Forest

This hike combines many attractive features: open views of Castle Crags and other nearby mountains, clear and cold streams cascading over granite boulders, and a 40-foot waterfall. You can access the trail all year; Burstarse Falls is largest and most impressive in spring. Note that it takes a bit of cross-country scrambling to actually visit the falls.

Reach the I-5 Castle Crags/Castella Exit 6 miles south of Dunsmuir and 48 miles north of Redding. Go west for 3.2 miles on Castle Creek Road, then park in the large open space on the right (known as Dog Trailhead).

Start at the parking area's northwest edge. You'll gain most of your elevation in the first part of the hike, so get the thighs pumping. A grove of knobcone pines quickly gives you an excuse to stop and examine the trees' tightly glued cones. This rugged species can often eke out an exist-ence in poor soil conditions that exclude other trees. As if this hardship were not enough, the cones will only release seeds after a fire.

Continue uphill through open chaparral slopes, pausing occasionally for more rest and southward views of Castle Creek Valley, Flume Creek Ridge, and Grey Rocks.

Reach the Pacific Crest Trail at 0.6 mile. Turn right, climb a bit more, then drop down to the soothing waters of Sulphur Creek, a good place to picnic and soak your feet. Like all the streams encountered on this trip,

The isolated spires of Castle Crags tower above the trail to Sulphur Creek and Burstarse Falls.

Sulphur Creek begins life high above in the granite peaks of Castle Crags.

Return 0.6 mile to the junction and continue straight. The trail rises gently as it travels a mile past Douglas firs, ponderosa pines, incense cedars, and black oaks to Popcorn Spring. Here you can rest in the shade of bigleaf maples and black oaks.

Burstarse Creek awaits another 0.8 mile up the trail. Continue 0.3 mile to Ugly Creek and then go 0.1 mile farther to where the path makes a 180-degree turn. Here you'll leave the path and descend the slope to Burstarse Creek (watch for poison oak). Head upstream 100 yards to the falls and the seclusion of its steep-walled canyon. This peaceful spot invites you to relax and merge with the mixture of unmoving rock and raining water.

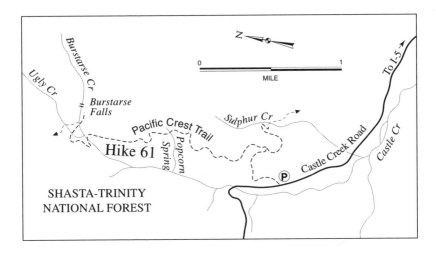

62 TWIN LAKES AND TAMARACK LAKE

Length: 3 miles round trip
Hiking time: 2 hours
High point: 6,600 feet
Total elevation gain: 800 feet
Difficulty: moderate
Season: mid-June to mid-October
Water: available from lakes; purify first
Map: USGS 7.5' Chicken Hawk Hill
Permit: none required
Nearest campground: Castle Crags State Park Campground
Information: Mount Shasta Ranger District, Shasta-Trinity National Forest

This trip gives you all you could hope for in a high-altitude hike: lush meadows; mixed forests that harbor multitudes of wildlife; big, beautiful lakes that beckon you to swim, fish, or meditate; and a high ridge that gives expansive views in all directions. Overnight camping was banned in and around this area for the 1995 summer season; this ban may continue in the future. Call the Mount Shasta Ranger District for current regulations if you plan on more than a day hike.

Take the I-5 Castella/Castle Crags Exit (6 miles south of Dunsmuir and 48 miles north of Redding) and go west on paved Castle Creek Road (also named Road 25 and Whalan Road). Crest a divide at 11

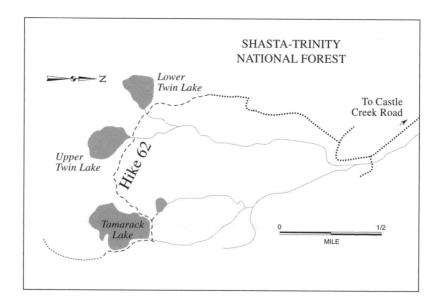

miles, stay left at 11.9 miles, then leave Road 25 for the left-forking dirt Road 38N17. Go 3 miles, then bear right at a fork for the final mile to the trailhead. This last stretch is rough on two-wheel drive vehicles, so if you're driving one, consider parking near or above the last fork and walking.

The south-running path begins near several campsites at the trailhead and immediately borders a green meadow filled with summer wildflowers. Grey Rocks and Flume Creek Ridge provide a scenic mountain background. Pass through a marsh, cross a small creek, then reach Lower Twin Lake at 0.4 mile. Though attractive, this shallow lake doesn't compare with its sibling awaiting farther up the trail, so continue on through the pine/fir forest to Upper Twin Lake. Here you'll find good summer swimming, places to camp, and a view of a nearby ridge.

When you're ready for different scenery, head east over the ridge

Corn lily is a common sight in high mountain meadows.

and drop to the shores of Tamarack Lake, the largest in the basin, which lies 1 mile from the trailhead. Visit the pond near its northwest edge, then follow the path near campsites on the east shore.

Mosey over to the meadows just above the southeast portion of the lake, where you'll find a small creek and numerous flowers. A faint trail guides you up to the ridge spine, which scintillates with a bright assortment of metamorphic rocks.

But the view can hold your attention for years. Immediately to the north are the three lakes, with Flume Creek Ridge and Grey Rocks just beyond. Farther in the distance, Castle Crags' granite spires scrape the sky, with Mount Eddy and attendants anchoring the far northern horizon. The metamorphic and granitic peaks of the Trinity Alps reign supreme to the west. To the south are range upon range of forested ridges, with the Sacramento Valley disappearing into distant haze. Lassen Peak and other Cascade volcanoes rise to the southeast, with more tree-clad mountains filling in the eastward vista.

63 BLACK BUTTE

Length: 5.2 miles round trip
Hiking time: 4 hours
High point: 6,325 feet
Total elevation gain: 1,850 feet
Difficulty: moderate
Season: mid-May through mid-November
Water: none; bring at least 1 quart per person
Map: USGS 7.5' City of Mount Shasta
Permit: none required
Nearest campground: McBride Springs Campground
Information: Mount Shasta Ranger District, Shasta-Trinity National Forest

Appearing imposingly steep from I-5, Black Butte has a moderately sloping trail curling around it that allows you to win its commanding summit views of Mount Shasta, Mount Eddy, and other massive mountains with a surprisingly modest effort.

From I-5, take the Central Mount Shasta exit. Go east 0.7 mile through town on Lake Street, then swing left onto Everitt Memorial Highway. Continue another 2.2 miles, then turn left at the Black Butte Trail sign onto a dirt road. Drive 0.1 mile, turn right, drive 1 mile, then curve 90 degrees and go straight towards Black Butte. Reach a road fork after another 0.3 mile, and go right (north). Drive 1.2 miles and turn left when you pass under a power line. From here, it's 0.7 mile to the trailhead, a small turnaround at the end of the road.

At the beginning, ponderosa pines, incense cedars, Douglas firs, and white firs offer partial shade for you and an understory of bush chinquapin, tobacco brush, and other shrubs. You'll soon have fine northward views of Weed directly below, with the sculpted hills of Shasta

The foundation of an old forest service lookout on the summit of Black Butte

Valley just beyond. Mount McLoughlin, a Cascade cousin of Mount Shasta, beckons from southern Oregon.

The path continues climbing at a steady rate along the sides of the young plug-dome volcano, which formed a little less than 10,000 years ago when four separate eruptions squeezed thick, viscous lava 2,300 feet above the surrounding plain.

Start a slow curve south at 1.1 miles and gain the first expansive vista to the west. The extensive bulk of the Klamath Mountains spreads

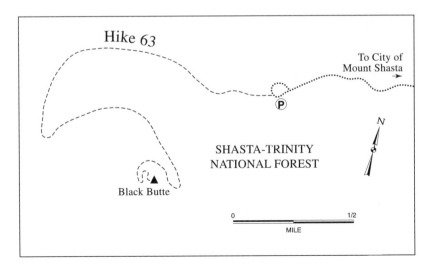

Hike 63

To City of
Mount Shasta
→

ⓅP

N

SHASTA-TRINITY
NATIONAL FOREST

Black Butte

0   1/2
MILE

before you. I-5 below is roughly the dividing line between the Cascades to the east and the Klamaths to the west. Thus, Mount Eddy to the southwest and Castle Crags to the south stand near the Klamaths' eastern boundary.

Farther up, the trail tends eastward at 1.6 miles as the snowy shoulders of Shastina and the rest of Mount Shasta's western flanks come into view. Western white pines, red firs, and mountain hemlocks stud the slopes as southern Cascade volcanoes Lassen Peak and Magee Peak appear to the southeast.

The path then snakes around to switchback up the western side to the summit. All the previous views now combine in a dazzling array of panoramic beauty that can keep you transfixed for hours.

64 CASTLE LAKE, HEART LAKE, AND MOUNT BRADLEY RIDGE

Length: 7 miles round trip
Hiking time: 5 hours or 2 days
High point: 6,050 feet
Total elevation gain: 1,300 feet
Difficulty: moderate
Season: mid-May through late October
Water: available from lakes; purify first
Maps: USGS 7.5' Seven Lakes Basin, USGS 7.5' Dunsmuir, USFS Castle Crags Wilderness
Permit: none required
Nearest campground: Castle Lake Campground
Information: Mount Shasta Ranger District, Shasta-Trinity National Forest

This hike features gorgeous alpine lakes, verdant mountain meadows, and a sweeping view of northern California's prominent peaks, with magnificent Mount Shasta easily winning top honors for most beautiful and most breathtaking. The majority of people do this trip as a day hike, but it's possible to camp amidst the granite surrounding Heart Lake or deep in the red fir forest on the way to Mount Bradley Ridge.

Take the Central Mount Shasta exit off I-5. Go west and south, first on South Old Stage Road, then on W. A. Barr Road. Cross Lake Siskiyou's dam 2.6 miles from the freeway, continue another 0.2 mile, then turn left onto the paved road that travels 7.1 miles to the parking area at Castle Lake.

Head for the six highly informative signboards that detail Castle Lake's natural history and the way humans have studied and manipulated the lake. Take a swim in the lake if it's a hot day, then cross the outlet creek and look for a trail sign that directs you uphill. Begin a steep climb on rocky tread as you enjoy vistas of the stony heights of

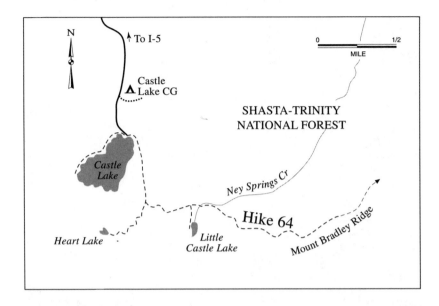

Castle Lake's glacial cirque and the intense sapphire of the lake's deep waters.

Continue past white and red firs to a saddle at 0.6 mile. About 100 feet before reaching a shallow seasonal pond, turn right (south) and follow an unmarked trail over rock slabs and up through a small meadow to reach Heart Lake at 1.1 miles. This tiny lake is aptly named: A small peninsula juts into the east edge to add the finishing touch to the heart shape. Head over to the outlet for a fantastic view down upon Castle Lake and beyond to Mount Shasta and Black Butte. If you walk past the lodgepole pines, western white pines, and red firs near the north and west shores, you'll see a couple of level areas that would make middling to poor campsites. A small pond is nestles just above the lake. The lake can be relatively warm in late summer's late afternoons: Dip in at the peninsula.

Return to the main trail at 1.6 miles and descend steeply through a rocky gully to another meadow at 2 miles. Take the unmarked side path that travels briefly to the very shallow and chaparral-encircled Little Castle Lake. Its most attractive aspect is the reflection of Mount Shasta from just above the southern shore.

Back on the trail, cross the outlet stream at 2.2 miles, ignore a faint side path to the right just beyond, speed downhill, then enter an open forest flush with regal red firs. Look to the right at 2.8 miles for an excellent campsite amidst the trees, descend a bit, then climb steeply to crest Mount Bradley Ridge at a saddle at 3.3 miles. Head another 0.2 mile left (northeast) to the nearest knob, then sit back and enjoy the panorama.

And what a panorama it is: The raw and jagged canines of the north section of Castle Crags rise abruptly just a mile to the south; nearby

Lodgepole pines frame a view of Castle Lake and the southern ridge of its glacial cirque.

Girard Ridge is the forefront for a distant eastward view of Lassen Peak, Magee Peak, Burney Mountain, and a plethora of other Cascade dignitaries; and Mount Shasta, Black Butte, and Mount Eddy rightfully command your respect and attention from the north.

When you leave this magic spot and return to Castle Lake, consider extending your hike by taking the half-mile trail that leaves the northeast end of the parking lot and runs along the east side of Castle Lake.

65 SEVEN LAKES BASIN

Length: 6 miles round trip
Hiking time: 5 hours or 2 days
High point: 6,900 feet
Total elevation gain: 1,250 feet
Difficulty: moderate
Season: early June through late October
Water: available only at Seven Lakes Basin; purify first; bring your own
Maps: USGS 7.5' Mumbo Basin, USGS 7.5' Seven Lakes Basin
Permit: none required
Nearest campground: Gumboot Campground
Information: Mount Shasta Ranger District, Shasta-Trinity National Forest

The walk to Seven Lakes Basin combines superb long-range vistas, gorgeous flower displays, and excellent swimming opportunities. It makes a great day hike, but backpackers will find spots to camp, either on high ridges or near water in the Seven Lakes Basin.

Take the Central Mount Shasta exit off I-5. Go west and south, first on South Old Stage Road and then on W. A. Barr Road, as you curve around Lake Siskiyou and meet Road 26. Follow 26 west (it's paved the whole way) along the South Fork Sacramento River, then park at Gumboot Saddle, which is 18.3 miles from Mount Shasta City and 2.5 miles west of the turnoff to Gumboot Lake and Gumboot Campground.

Head to the south side of Gumboot Saddle and begin walking south on the Pacific Crest Trail, a 2,600-mile path that snakes through some of the most beautiful country of California, Oregon, and Washington.

You'll quickly pass the PCT trail register, then climb to the first good viewpoint. Look west at the stony spines of the Trinity Alps, home to granitic and metamorphic spires. To the south and north stretch range upon range of the Trinity Divide's forested slopes.

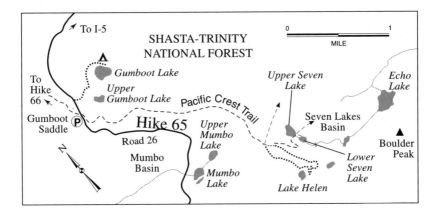

Snags litter the shoreline of Upper Seven Lake.

The trail begins a series of gentle undulations along the ridge. Jeffrey pines, western white pines, and red and white firs provide some shade for you and an understory of pinemat and greenleaf manzanita, currant, squaw carpet, blue lupines, yellow sulfur flowers, and numerous other plants.

Look for a good campsite on the left at 0.3 mile. Near here, you'll catch the first good look northeast of the steep flanks and snow-swept summit of Mount Shasta, the visual and spiritual anchor of northern California. As you continue, the panorama expands to include Mount Eddy to the north and Gumboot Lake just below to the east. Also note Mumbo Lake and Mumbo Basin downhill to the southwest.

Reach a saddle with a trail fork at 2.4 miles. Here you complete the hike's survey of northern California landmarks by studying faraway Lassen Peak, Magee Peak, and Burney Mountain rising high to the southeast. Nearer are Flume Ridge and Grey Rocks in the same direction, with the granite cliffs of Castle Crags punctuating the horizon due east. Seven Lakes Basin lies just below. Upper Seven Lake and Lower Seven Lake nestle up to the ridge upon which you stand. Farther east, Boulder Peak stands guard over Echo Lake.

For the quickest route down to the basin, ignore the signs and head left 30 feet on the PCT. Look for a faint, unmarked trail on the right, follow it down to its intersection with a four-wheel-drive road, then take the road left to the shores of Upper Seven Lake for a total distance of a half mile. For a longer, gentler descent, take the right-hand trail, which connects with four-wheel-drive roads to reach the same destination.

Upper Seven Lake's deep and clear waters invite a refreshing swim. Two campsites are too near the water, so look farther away for a level spot. Lower Seven Lake, 100 yards south, has no campsites.

Feel free to wander cross-country in the basin. The trail grows fainter as it heads east to Echo Lake. Although the beauty of this lake and Boulder Peak just above will certainly tempt you to visit, the lake is under private ownership. The owner, very persnickety about private property rights, doesn't take kindly to strangers nosing about "his" land.

66 PACIFIC CREST TRAIL TO PORCUPINE LAKE AND THE DEADFALL LAKES

Length: 23 miles round trip
Hiking time: 3 to 4 days
High point: 7,650 feet
Total elevation gain: 2,150 feet
Difficulty: moderate
Season: late June through mid-October
Water: sporadically available; purify first; always have at least 1 quart per person on hand
Maps: USGS 7.5' South China Mtn., USGS 7.5' Mumbo Basin, USGS 7.5' Seven Lakes Basin, USGS 7.5' Mount Eddy
Permit: none required
Nearest campground: Gumboot Campground
Information: Mount Shasta Ranger District, Shasta-Trinity National Forest

This walk along the Pacific Crest Trail features exhilarating views of major northern California landmarks ranging from Lassen Peak to Mount Shasta to Mount Eddy to the Trinity Alps and other Klamath Mountain ranges. You'll also visit Porcupine Lake, pass by meadows and springs, and walk near the head of a glacial cirque with an amazing display of wildflowers. In addition, you can easily connect with hike 67 trails to explore the Deadfall Lakes region and climb Mount Eddy.

From I-5, take the Central Mount Shasta Exit. Head west and south, first on South Old Stage Road and then on W. A. Barr Road.

Bend around Lake Siskiyou to meet Road 26. Follow 26 west (it's paved the whole way) along the South Fork Sacramento River, then park at Gumboot Saddle, which is 18.3 miles from Mount Shasta City and 2.5 miles west of the turnoff to Gumboot Lake and Gumboot Campground.

Find the path on the east side of the large parking lot and start climbing, soon enjoying a good southwest view of the Trinity Alps as you walk through a forest of Jeffrey and western white pine and white and red fir. The western white pines and red firs will be with you for much of the journey, being replaced only at the higher elevations by mountain hemlock and whitebark pine.

Gain another view at 0.4 mile, this time of mighty Mount Shasta, the drainage of the South Fork Sacramento River, Gumboot Lake, and many nearby mountains. Thus begins a pattern that will last for several miles: ascending and descending moderately as the trail alternates between the west and east sides of the north-running ridge crest.

Cross a dirt road at 0.7 mile, and then at 1 mile look north to Mount Eddy and west down to Picayune Lake. A saddle at 1.6 miles frames a view of Mount Shasta and a level spot for camping. Such spots are interspersed along much of the trail, except for the last section from Toad Lake to the Deadfall Lakes.

Another saddle at 2.7 miles holds a trail junction. Continue straight and climb, soon reaching a series of spring-fed and flower-festooned meadows that stretch west down the mountainside (one spring flows year-round). Return to the east side of the crest and walk by more meadows and a thick red fir forest, then enter open country at 5.6 miles with an expansive vista southeast to Lassen Peak and its neighboring volcanoes.

Reach a trail fork at 6.1 miles and go left, leaving the Pacific Crest Trail for a brief 0.2-mile climb to Porcupine Lake. Surrounded by the high rock walls of its glacial cirque, this beautiful lake has deep, clear waters for swimming and several campsites near the eastern shore. It makes an excellent first-day destination.

Return to the PCT and walk 0.2 mile to another trail fork at 6.3 miles. You can take a right and drop 0.4 mile down to the west shore of

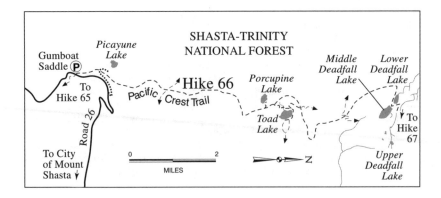

attractive Toad Lake, where you'll find several good campsites. The trail then rises from the lake's northwest edge to rejoin the PCT.

If you don't visit Toad Lake, continue along the PCT, contour above Toad Lake and enjoy stupendous views to the east and south. Go straight when the trail from Toad Lake crosses the PCT at 7.2 miles, then climb up to a saddle, the trip's highest elevation, at 8 miles. Say good-bye to southern views and hello to Mount Eddy, which rises prominently 2 miles to the north. You now contour along a large glacial cirque that heads the North Fork Sacramento River drainage. Note the intense trailside display of dozens of wildflower species.

Reach another saddle and a trail fork at 9.2 miles. Go briefly left for 50 feet, then go right at another fork on the higher of two trails that leave from the saddle's western side. Enjoy the vista of the Klamath Mountains as you gently descend past red firs, flowers, a few meadows, and talus boulder slopes to see Lower Deadfall Lake at 10.8 miles.

Continue down to a trail fork at 11.3 miles. A right quickly brings you to campsites at impressively beautiful Middle Deadfall Lake. To finish this hike and to connect with hike 67, go left for the final 0.2 mile to a meeting of trails at Deadfall Creek.

A view of Mount Shasta from the Pacific Crest Trail above Toad Lake

67 DEADFALL LAKES AND MOUNT EDDY

Length: 10 miles round trip
Hiking time: 6 hours or 2 days
High point: 9,025 feet
Total elevation gain: 2,250 feet
Difficulty: moderate to difficult
Season: early July through mid-October
Water: available from lakes and streams; purify first; have at least 1 quart per person when climbing past Upper Deadfall Lake
Maps: USGS 7.5' South China Mtn., USGS 7.5' Mount Eddy
Permit: none required
Nearest campground: McBride Springs Campground
Information: Mount Shasta Ranger District, Shasta-Trinity National Forest

This hike has something for everybody: Families with young ones can easily make the gentle climb to Lower and Middle Deadfall lakes, with or without backpacks; hard-core hikers will delight both in the lungburn from Upper Deadfall Lake to the summit of Mount Eddy and in Eddy's top-of-the-world views; and botanists and amateur plant lovers will be ecstatic over the incredible diversity of flowers and trees found along the trail. Note that you also have the option to connect with hikes 66 and 68 for much longer excursions; taking hike 66 south as far as Toad Lake and Porcupine Lake would be your best bet.

To reach the trailhead, take I-5's Edgewood/Gazelle Exit just north of Weed. Pass under the freeway, go right at the stop sign, then go 0.3 mile farther and turn left onto Stewart Springs Road. The road crosses Parks Creek at Stewart Springs and changes names to Road 17. Follow it 13.4 miles to a saddle above Parks Creek and park in the large lot on the left.

Start a gentle ascent on the Pacific Crest Trail with the company of red firs, white firs, and Jeffrey and western white pines. Soon the forest opens to allow magnificent vistas of the Trinity Alps to the southwest, with much of the rest of the Klamath Mountains filling out the remainder of the western horizon. Pass by a plethora of wildflowers and glimpses of Deadfall Meadows to reach a stream at 1.1 miles, then another stream and bordering meadow at 2.1 miles.

A trail fork awaits at 2.6 miles near Deadfall Creek. Hike 66 follows the PCT straight and south. The path to the right runs 2 miles downhill to Deadfall Meadows, passing wet, wondrous, and abundant displays of meadow wildflowers along the way (it meets Road 17 a mile beyond this hike's trailhead). Either of these two options quickly accesses side trails that lead to Lower Deadfall Lake, which has a few campsites but loses much of its water by late summer.

Take the left-trending trail, then descend one of the side paths to the right that leads to stunning Middle Deadfall Lake. Here you'll see reddish-purple and gray-green ridges surrounding the deep and clear

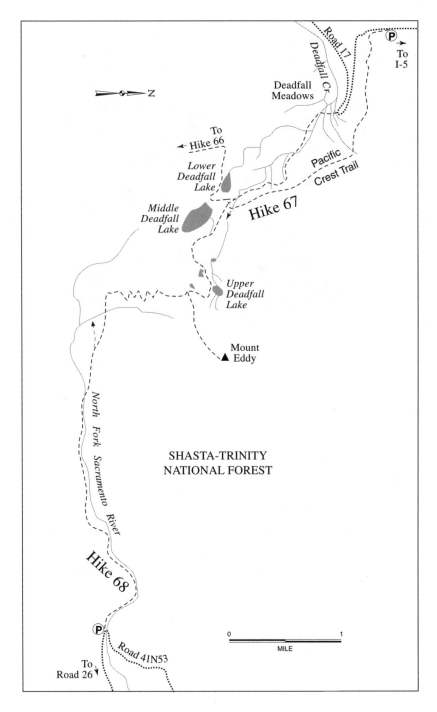

Young hikers gaze down at Upper Deadfall Lake from near the summit of Mount Eddy. (Photo by Marc J. Soares)

waters, which run from light green near the edges to dark blue in the middle. This is a great place to camp; look for sites near the north and west sides.

To complete the hike, continue up the main trail, reaching a warm pond at 3.4 miles that's great for swimming and is blessed by the presence of the rare (in northern California) foxtail pine, the quite common lodgepole pine, and an excellent view of the final destination: Mount Eddy. Continue another 0.2 mile to Upper Deadfall Lake, another stunner that offers good swimming and great views, along with spring-fed meadows on the east side.

The path then climbs in earnest, reaching Deadfall Summit at 4.2 miles, where you'll see hike 68 heading east (right) from the gap. Gather your energy and ambition, then start north (left) up the ridge for the final 0.8 mile to the summit of Mount Eddy (an older trail begins just down to the east).

Your ample reward is the 360-degree panorama over some of the most beautiful country in the world: northern California. Demanding homage and respect, Mount Shasta looms overwhelmingly to the east, easily dwarfing nearer Black Butte. The rest of the Cascades stretch southeast toward Lassen Peak and north to Mount McLaughlin. Due south are spiny Castle Crags and other peaks and ridges of the Trinity Divide. To the west, the Deadfall Lakes basin anchors a stupendous view of the Trinity Alps and the rest of the Klamath Mountains.

68

NORTH FORK SACRAMENTO RIVER TO DEADFALL SUMMIT

Length: 10.4 miles round trip
Hiking time: 7 hours or 2 days
High point: 8,020 feet
Total elevation gain: 2,750 feet
Difficulty: moderate to strenuous
Season: early July to mid-October
Water: available from the North Fork Sacramento River; purify first
Map: USGS 7.5' Mount Eddy
Permit: none required
Nearest campground: Gumboot Campground
Information: Mount Shasta Ranger District, Shasta-Trinity National Forest

Map on page 173

This journey appeals most to those who feel a sense of adventure and excitement in making their way along an historic path that is occasionally difficult to follow. It is also a journey for those in fairly good shape, for although the path rises moderately for the first 3.7 miles, it will jam your knees into your teeth on the final push to the saddle above Deadfall Lakes (Deadfall Summit). This hike connects with hike 67, which leads to hike 66, and thus allows you to arrange a car shuttle. You'd be smarter, though, to do either hike 66 or 67 first, then coast downhill to this hike's trailhead.

Take I-5's Central Mount Shasta exit, then go west and south on South Old Stage Road and W. A. Barr Road. Swing around Lake Siskiyou's southwest shore to Road 26. Travel 5.3 miles to a crossing of the South Fork Sacramento River, then turn left 0.1 mile farther onto Road 41N53, which is signed for Toad Lake and Morgan Meadows. Bear right at a road fork at 0.2 mile, cross a cement bridge over the Middle Fork Sacramento River at 0.7 mile, then continue on 41N53 another 3.2 miles. Park on the right side of the road just before the cement bridge crossing the North Fork Sacramento River.

Cross the road and, facing upstream, start hiking up the left side of the river. You're now on the Sisson-Callahan National Recreation Trail, which has its origins in the mid-1800s when trappers, prospectors, and cattlemen made their way up the North Fork Sacramento River drainage; around 1911, the Forest Service extended it west to Callahan from "Sisson" (presently the town of Mount Shasta). Note the post that marks the trek's beginning; similar posts sporting the National Recreation Trail symbol will help guide you along the route. Look for these posts when the trail disappears, and remember that for the first 2.7 miles you'll walk near the south banks of the North Fork Sacramento River.

The North Fork Sacramento River near the Sisson-Callahan National Recreation Trail

White firs, Douglas firs, and incense cedars provide company as you climb above the tumbling cascades of the small river, cross a dirt road, then reach the first decent campsite at 1.1 miles (other level areas await farther along). Pass a spring and soon thereafter lose the trail briefly (follow a rocky gully through the meadow). Note the appearance of Jeffrey pines in the forest, then look north for views of a meadow across the river and then east for tree-filtered views of Mount Shasta. Join a dirt road at 1.7 miles for 0.2 mile, enter a meadow where the path dwindles, then climb up for more views at 2.6 miles of Mount Shasta, with the addition of Mount Eddy and its east-trending ridge.

Cross the North Fork Sacramento River 0.1 mile farther (look for a post on the north side) and make your way westward past extensive meadows that provide a year-round home for lodgepole pines and a seasonal home for grasses, wildflowers, and a few cattle. Red fir and western white pine become the dominant tree species before you reach a junction with an extremely faint trail at 3.7 miles. Go right on the main trail, following tree blazes and rock ducks when necessary.

The way soon swings northward and grows much steeper as you switchback up through forest. As you near the gap and the meeting with hike 67 at 5.2 miles, enjoy southeasterly views of distant Lassen Peak and the Northern Sierra Nevada, in addition to southern vistas of nearer mountains. You'll also see the Pacific Crest Trail (hike 66) contouring along the steep mountainside just to the south.

Lava Beds National Monument

The entrance to Big Painted Cave, which harbors ancient Indian pictographs

69 BUNCHGRASS TRAIL

Length: 2 miles round trip
Hiking time: 1.5 hours, day hike only
High point: 4,750 feet
Total elevation gain: 150 feet
Difficulty: easy
Season: mid-April through mid-November
Water: none; bring your own
Map: USGS 7.5' Lava Beds National Monument
Permit: none required
Nearest campground: Indian Well Campground
Information: Lava Beds National Monument

The Bunchgrass Trail, conveniently located for those staying in the campground or wanting a hike near the visitor center, is an easy stroll on a wide dirt road that offers both good views and solitude.

Enter Indian Well Campground, which is across the road from the visitor center and 9.7 miles south of the Hill Road/Lava Beds National Monument Road junction. Descend 0.4 mile, turn left for the B-loop, then park across from the rest rooms near campsites 14, 15, and 16.

Start by site B-7 at the campground's northwest edge. Almost immediately, you'll spy a lone ponderosa pine 100 feet to the right. This species typically requires 20 to 25 inches of rain annually for survival, much more than Lava Beds National Monument usually receives. This pine must have good access to underground moisture, something that's difficult to achieve in the porous volcanic soils of the region.

Note the large quantities of native bunchgrass as you continue. Competition from nonnative grasses and past cattle grazing diminished the quantity of this plant, but recent burns have led to its resurgence here. You'll also see sagebrush, rabbitbrush, antelopebrush, and western juniper.

Northward vistas of Schonchin Butte, Gillem Bluff and Mount Dome appear between western junipers, as do westward views of nearby Crescent Butte on the left. Several mountain mahoganies line the trail at 0.3 mile, followed by a view of Hippo Butte to the west.

Climb gently at 0.5 mile and begin approaching Lava Beds National Monument Road. At 0.9 mile, the dirt road turns to trail, passes through an open hillside covered with native bunchgrass, then reaches the scenic overlook at Lava Beds National Monument Road at 1 mile.

The overlook allows excellent views; look for Mount Dome, Gillem Bluff, Devil's Homestead Lava Flow, Schonchin Butte, Schonchin Lava Flow, and Tule Lake to the north; small cinder cones, open lands, and the distant Warner Mountains to the east; Crescent Butte, other cinder cones, and the highlands of the Medicine Lake volcano to the south; and Hippo Butte, Bearpaw Butte, Whitney Butte, and the Callahan Lava Flow to the west. You'll also find two informational signs: One describes

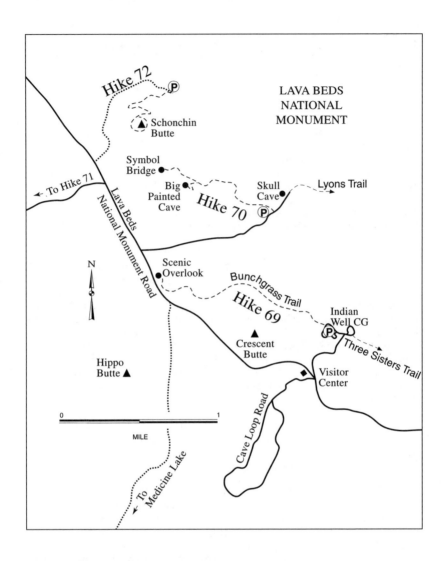

the wide variety of animal life that makes this region home; the other discusses air quality and the various factors affecting visibility.

Those who wish to do the hike one way can be dropped off or picked up here. The pickup spot is 1.1 miles north of the visitor center (8.6 miles south of the Hill Road/Lava Beds National Monument Road junction).

Nearby: Experienced hikers with a strong desire to penetrate the far reaches of Lava Beds National Monument's backcountry should consider hiking the Three Sisters Trail, which begins from Loop A in the

A view from the Bunchgrass Trail of rabbitbrush, bunchgrass, western junipers, and distant Mount Dome

Indian Well Campground. The path swings around to Skull Cave, a total distance of 8.7 miles. But check in first at the visitor center for orientation and safety precautions.

And no visitor to Lava Beds National Monument should miss exploring one or more of the subterranean passages accessible from Cave Loop Road. Go underground (on foot and sometimes on hands, knees, or belly) through an enticing assortment of colorfully named lava tube caves: Golden Dome, Hopkins Chocolate, Blue Grotto, Hercules' Leg. Stop by the visitor center to borrow flashlights and buy hard hats and also to gain intimate knowledge of lava tube cave geology and features by touring Mushpot Cave, which has lighted trail and informational signs. When caving, always remember to go with someone else; tell others where you're going; carry at least three sources of light; wear a hard hat, jacket, pants, and sturdy shoes; stay on trails when they exist; keep from damaging rock formations; and quietly leave any cave with bats.

70 SYMBOL BRIDGE AND BIG PAINTED CAVE

Length: 1.6 miles round trip
Hiking time: 1.5 hours, day hike only
High point: 4,700 feet
Total elevation gain: 100 feet
Difficulty: easy
Season: mid-April through mid-November
Water: none; bring your own
Map: USGS 7.5' Lava Beds National Monument
Permit: none required
Nearest campground: Indian Well Campground
Information: Lava Beds National Monument

Map on page 180

This short and level hike provides an easy way to explore some of Lava Beds National Monument's less-visited caves. Two of these caves bear ancient Indian pictographs.

Drive Lava Beds National Monument Road 1.6 miles north of the visitor center (8.1 miles south of the Hill Road/Lava Beds National Monument Road junction). Turn east at the sign for Skull Cave and go 1 mile to the small parking area on the left.

The path initially heads straight for the sparsely vegetated, steep-sided southern flanks of Schonchin Butte. Look for the aptly named bunchgrass dotting the landscape, along with sharp-scented sagebrush, rabbitbrush, antelopebrush, bitter cherry, and western juniper. Views include numerous cinder cones and the Medicine Lake volcano to the west and south, and the Warner Mountains on the skyline far to the east.

At 0.3 mile, you'll cross a deep trench up to 40 feet deep and 60 feet wide that's littered with jagged chunks of dark-colored volcanic basalt ranging in size from baseballs to cars. This trench is part of a lava tube system. Lava tubes form from flows of erupted liquid basalt. As the outer edge of a flow cools, the inner, hotter lava continues to stream, leaving a hollow tunnel behind. All of the more than 300 caves in Lava Beds National Monument (most around 30,000 years old) are sections of lava tubes.

What you see on both sides is a collapsed section of the Modoc Crater Lava Tube System, which begins at Modoc Crater about 2 miles southwest; passes through Merrill Cave, Symbol Bridge, Big Painted Cave, and Skull Cave; and then ends near Tule Lake's old shoreline. You can easily explore underneath the "bridge" that allows the trail to cross the trench.

The path parallels the trench, then reaches a short, left-running trail at 0.4 mile to the edge of the trench. You'll find the trail to Big Painted Cave 0.2 mile farther, but save this adventure for the way back and for now continue another 0.2 mile to Symbol Bridge.

Symbol Bridge is a holy Indian site; enter it with respect and an open heart. The trail drops down to the entrance just below a large, multitrunked western juniper. Move into the dimly lit interior and let your eyes adjust to the attenuated light. Careful inspection will reveal Indian pictographs on rocks on both sides of the cave entrance. Think of those who created them and of the many generations who came after. Do not touch the pictographs; skin oils can damage them.

You can hike all the way through the cool air under the bridge to the opening on the other sde (bring flashlights), but you'll have to return the way you came. Note the many colors of the rocks: dark reddish-brown, pink, purple-gray, and green.

After imbibing the essence of Symbol Bridge, head back and take the short path to Big Painted Cave. Use your familiarity with the pictographs at Symbol Bridge to help you locate the much fainter ones in Big Painted Cave. Only experienced cavers should attempt the narrow passage at the back of cave. The cave on the opposite side of this tube-collapse system also merits exploration.

Those who enter any cave should follow these rules: Tell someone where you're going; don't go alone; wear a hard hat, sturdy shoes, a jacket, and pants; carry at least three sources of light; don't damage rock formations; where trails exist, stay on them; leave a cave quietly if you encounter bats.

Nearby: Continue 0.1 mile down the road from the trailhead to Skull Cave. This large cave, named for the numerous animals and two humans that died in a pit inside, has been developed to make exploration easy. The Lyons Trail, which leaves from the Skull Cave parking lot, allows adventurous backpackers to explore the wildest areas of Lava Beds National Monument. Anyone considering such a trip must first check in at the visitor center for orientation and safety precautions.

71 WHITNEY BUTTE

Length: 6.8 miles round trip
Hiking time: 5 hours or 2 days
High point: 5,010 feet
Total elevation gain: 500 feet
Difficulty: moderate
Season: mid-April through mid-November
Water: none; bring your own
Map: USGS 7.5' Lava Beds National Monument
Permit: none required
Nearest campground: Indian Well Campground
Information: Lava Beds National Monument

The trip to the top of Whitney Butte offers the best of Lava Beds National Monument: wildlife, open vistas of Northeastern California,

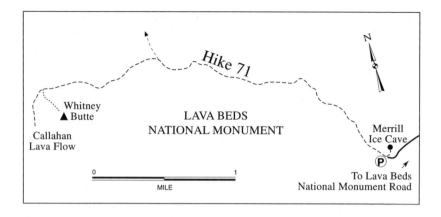

up-close views of volcanic land forms, and backpacking opportunities for the adventurous.

Drive Lava Beds National Monument Road 2.1 miles north of the visitor center (7.6 miles south of the Hill Road/Lava Beds National Monument Road junction). Turn west at the sign for Merrill Cave and go 0.8 mile to the parking area.

If you're a backpacker, remember the following: Bring all water with you (at least 2 quarts per person per day); fires are always prohibited, and even gas stoves may be prohibited during times of high fire danger; camp at least 1 mile from the trailhead and public roads (there are no developed sites, but you'll find numerous flat areas); the maximum group size is twelve; leave pets and firearms at home. Of course, all hikers should wear wide-brimmed hats and good sun protection.

The path to Whitney Butte begins in a northwest direction, slowly descending through a landscape dotted with sagebrush, antelopebrush, rabbitbrush, and mountain mahogany. Western juniper is by far the most common tree, but you'll also spot a few ponderosa pines. Look north for views of the Devil's Homestead Lava Flow, Gillem Bluff, Tule Lake, Mount Dome, and distant Mount McLoughlin in southern Oregon. To the east rises Schonchin Butte, which, like Whitney Butte, is a cinder cone.

The trail bends westward at 1.8 miles, allowing the first view of the broad flanks and high summit of Mount Shasta. Go left at a trail fork at 2.2 miles, continue west, then eventually border the northern edge of Whitney Butte.

After rounding Whitney Butte, the trail continues another 0.1 mile to end at the edge of Callahan Lava Flow. This massive sheet of basalt covers many square miles and was extruded from Cinder Butte to the south around 1,100 years ago. Note that lichens and a few plants have begun the slow process of colonizing the edge of the flow.

To reach the summit of Whitney Butte, retrace your steps to a ponderosa pine growing where the trail bends and where you had your first good views of the Callahan Lava Flow on the way in. From here,

On Whitney Butte, mountain mahogany and sagebrush border a southwesterly vista that includes Mount Shasta.

pick your own route to the top of the cinder cone, where excellent views in all directions await.

Nearby: Merrill Cave, reached by a short paved trail from the parking lot, ranks as one of the most spectacular in Lava Beds National Monument. It's part f the Modoc Crater Lava Tube System, which begins at Modoc Crater about 0.8 mile due south and stretches 10 miles northeast to the old shoreline of Tule Lake. From the trail's end, you'll descend a 15-foot stairway, travel through the cave, then descend a 17-foot ladder to the cave's lower chamber. Here you'll find a small lake that's frozen year-round. As in some other caves in the monument, ice forms here because cold air sinks into the cave in winter, cooling the cave to below freezing temperatures. Percolating precipitation from the surface and moisture from the air collect in the bottom of the cave as ice. If you enter Merrill Cave, remember the following: Don't go alone; tell someone where you're going; carry at least three sources of light; wear sturdy shoes, a hard hat, a jacket, pants, and gloves; don't damage rock formations; where trails exist, stay on them; leave quietly if you encounter bats.

72 SCHONCHIN BUTTE

Length: 1.5 miles round trip
Hiking time: 1.5 hours, day hike only
High point: 5,253 feet
Total elevation gain: 450 feet
Difficulty: moderate
Season: mid-April through mid-November
Water: none; bring your own
Map: USGS 7.5' Lava Beds National Monument
Permit: none required
Nearest campground: Indian Well Campground
Information: Lava Beds National Monument

Map on page 180

The hike to the summit of Schonchin Butte offers many rewards: an abundance of flowers in late spring and early summer; expansive vistas of Lava Beds National Monument and surrounding northeastern California landmarks; and a steady, moderate trail gradient that allows you to set a satisfying climbing pace matched to your body's rhythms.

Drive Lava Beds National Monument Road 2.2 miles north of the visitor center (7.4 miles south of the Hill Road/Lava Beds National Monument Road junction). Head 1.1 miles on the dirt road to the parking area (leave room for others to turn around).

The ascent begins in a plant community consisting primarily of seasonal flowers, antelopebrush, rabbitbrush, sagebrush, bitter cherry, mountain mahogany, and western juniper. Almost immediately, a short side trail on the right leads to a small cave about 6 feet deep. Enjoy northward views as you continue on the main path.

At 0.2 mile, a bench invites you to take a breather. Note the relative profusion of plant life here on the north side of Schonchin Butte as compared to the south side; the northern slopes receive less sun and can therefore retain more moisture for nourishing plants.

The first switchback and a good view of Mount Shasta await at 0.4 mile, followed 0.1 mile farther by another trailside bench shaded by two western juniper trees. Reach another switchback and then continue up to a trail fork just below the summit at 0.6 mile.

Head right and gain the butte's rim. Schonchin Butte, a cinder cone, formed over 30,000 years ago when a volcanic vent, in successive eruptions, shot lava into the air. Look around at the topography of Lava Beds National Monument and you'll see numerous other steep-sided cinder cones, which rarely exceed 1,000 feet in height.

Circumnavigate the rim over to the fire lookout. During fire season, you can visit with the person staffing the lookout if she or he is not busy and invites you in. Four signs, one on each side of the lookout, explain the geological history of the area and include maps of local landmarks.

The lookout offers commanding views. Immediately to the north stretches the Schonchin Lava Flow, which spreads from the base of Schonchin Butte to cover several square miles. Just west of Tule Lake is Gillem Bluff; three other fault escarpments, each higher than the last, rise to the northwest. Mount Dome is the nearest high mountain, with Mount McLoughlin beckoning in the far distance from southern Oregon.

Mount Shasta dominates the southwestern horizon. Much nearer, you'll see the black basalt of the Callahan Lava Flow, which oozed from nearby Cinder Butte. Whitney Butte and several other cinder cones also dot the landscape in this direction.

To the south, you'll see the highlands of the Medicine Lake volcano. Much of the lava in Lava Beds National Monument flowed northward from Mammoth Crater, a nearer but less prominent volcano.

Just below Schonchin Butte to the east, you'll see the collapsed lava

Schonchin Butte's crater and fire lookout

tube systems that house Skull, Symbol Bridge, and Big Painted caves. Beyond the caves are more cinder cones, with the distant Warner Mountains capping the horizon.

Nearby: Consider exploring Balcony Cave and Boulevard Cave, reached by a short trail that leaves the east side of Lava Beds National Monument Road 0.8 mile northwest of the turnoff to Schonchin Butte. Cavers should always observe the following rules: Tell others where you're going; go with someone else; carry at least three sources of light; wear a hard hat, jacket, pants, and sturdy shoes; stay on trails when they exist; keep from damaging rock formations; quietly leave any cave with bats.

73 BLACK CRATER/THOMAS-WRIGHT BATTLEFIELD

Length: 2.4 miles round trip
Hiking time: 2 hours, day hike only
High point: 4,400 feet
Total elevation gain: 150 feet
Difficulty: easy
Season: mid-April through mid-November
Water: none; bring your own
Map: USGS 7.5' Lava Beds National Monument
Permit: none required
Nearest campground: Indian Well Campground
Information: Lava Beds National Monument

This hike gives you the opportunity to study spatter cone geology up close at Black Crater. It also features an easy walk to the Thomas-Wright Battlefield, where interpretive signs give in-depth explanations of a Modoc Indian War battle and its outcome.

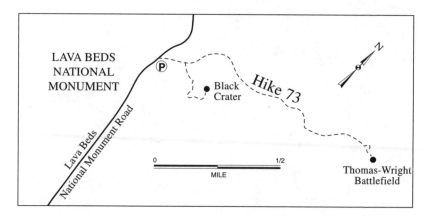

Devil's Homestead Lava Flow and Mount Dome

Drive Lava Beds National Monument Road 4.8 miles north of the visitor center (4.9 miles south of the Hill Road/Lava Beds National Monument Road junction). Park in the lot on the east side of the road.

As you leave the parking lot, note that an antelopebrush specimen grows on the left side of the "trail" sign, with rabbitbrush on the right. And on the left, 10 feet beyond the sign, is a western juniper tree, followed by sagebrush.

Walk 0.1 mile and turn right at a trail fork. Climb another 0.1 mile up and across chunky basalt to Black Crater. This is an excellent example of a spatter cone: Molten lava full of trapped gasses surged through a vent and burst through the surface here. Look around at the lava on the sides of the crater; it has the appearance of thick batter poured onto the ground. Also note the different colors the basalt rock has turned—plum, dark purple, orange-red—and the gold, green, and white crustose lichens that are gaining a foothold here.

In addition to offering your eyes a rainbow of rock colors, Black Crater gives an impressive 360-degree vista of northeastern California's terrain. Mount Shasta anchors the southwestern view, with Whitney Butte just to its left. To the south, look for nearby Hippo, Bearpaw, and Schonchin buttes, with the Medicine Lake volcano on the horizon. Near to the east is Hardin Butte and the Schonchin Lava Flow, with the Warner Mountains rising up near the Nevada border. Tule Lake, Devil's Homestead Lava Flow, Gillem Bluff and Mount Dome are prominent to the north.

Return to the trail fork and head right, being sure to sign in at the trail register that quickly appears on the right. The path slowly descends as it skirts the edge of a lava flow from Black Crater, then enters an area populated by fernbush. A bench shaded by a western juniper tree awaits about 0.3 mile from the trailhead. Just beyond, a sign discusses a tree mold: Liquid lava flowed around a tree trunk, then hardened.

Continue past chunks of lava, then cross an open area filled with native bunchgrass. Two informative signs soon appear: One describes the geological processes that formed the Tule Lake basin; the other points out landmarks visible to the south.

The trail ends 1.1 miles from the trailhead at the Thomas-Wright Battlefield. Two more signs discuss the battle between the U.S. Army forces, who left Gillem's Camp and entered the depression below, and Modoc Indians, who were hidden where you stand and at other nearby high places, and who launched a successful attack that killed or wounded two-thirds of the 68 soldiers.

Nearby: For a picnic in the shade of western juniper trees and the opportunity to study more geology, visit Fleener Chimneys (0.6 mile south from the trailhead, then west for 0.7 mile). Gillem Bluff, a major fault in the earth's crust, visible a few miles to the north, helped create these spatter-cone chimneys: Lava rose through the fault to surface here. One of the spatter-cone holes is about 50 feet deep. The Devil's Homestead Lava Flow, which stretches north from here for 3.5 miles, originated underneath Fleener Chimneys between 2,000 and 8,000 years ago.

74 GILLEM BLUFF

Length: 1.8 miles round trip
Hiking time: 2 hours, day hike only
High point: 4,500 feet
Total elevation gain: 450 feet
Difficulty: moderate
Season: mid-April through mid-November
Water: none; bring your own
Map: USGS 7.5' Lava Beds National Monument
Permit: none required
Nearest campground: Indian Well Campground
Information: Lava Beds National Monument

The steep climb up Gillem Bluff begins at a site of significant historical importance in the 1872–73 Modoc Indian War and ends with bird's-eye views of Lava Beds National Monument and much of northeastern California.

Drive Lava Beds National Monument Road 9.5 miles north of the visitor center (0.2 mile west of the Hill Road/Lava Beds National Monument Road junction) and park in the spacious lot at Gillem's Camp.

Begin your hiking by exploring Gillem's Camp. This spot served as the main headquarters for the U.S. Army during the 1872–73 Modoc

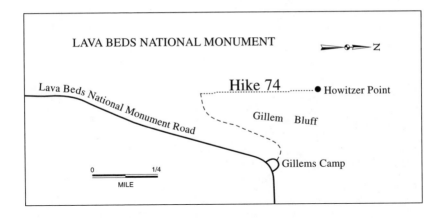

Indian War (informational signs give many of the details). Just west of the parking area look for a small cemetery that served as a temporary resting place for some of the U.S. soldiers killed in the war (all bodies have been removed). Just north of the parking area lies a circle of rocks, possibly intended by the military as a battle fortification.

Head uphill and begin the ascent of Gillem Bluff on an old road used by Modoc hunters for many centuries and by the army during the war to bring in supplies via mule. As views steadily improve, continue upward across an open slope that's dotted with antelopebrush, sagebrush, rabbitbrush, and western juniper and occasionally dominated by native bunchgrass.

At 0.6 mile, a rock outcrop beckons the weary to rest and enjoy the panorama. The trail then briefly levels as it passes rocks sporting orange, yellow, green, and brown crustose lichens.

Climb some more, then reach the end of the trail atop the bluff at 0.9 mile. Mount Shasta's 14,162-foot summit rises to the southwest, with nearer Mount Dome dominating the west; the entire expanse of Lava Beds National Monument stretches south below, with the Medicine Lake volcano commanding the southern skyline; the Warner Mountains scrape the sky to the east; and Tule Lake and fertile farm fields form the northeast vista. Adventurous hikers can climb north a half mile to the top of the bluff and gain the section of the northward view not available at the trail's end.

Nearby: Do some bird-watching at Tule Lake, which hosts nearly a million migratory geese and ducks by early November. However, a visit any time of the year will reward you with glimpses of many of the 250 bird species that live in or pass through the area. From Gillem's Camp, head 7.5 miles east on Lava Beds National Monument Road, then turn left for the auto tour route. This dirt road heads west and north to reach Hill Road 3.1 miles north of Lava Beds National Monument Road. Bring binoculars and a bird identification book. Also consider traveling 9.1 miles north up Hill Road to the visitor center on Tule Lake's west side; it

Gillem Bluff and the beginning of the Gillem Bluff Trail

houses a museum and wildlife displays. Call the visitor center at (916) 667-2231 for more information on Tule Lake and other Klamath Basin Wildlife Refuges.

75 CAPTAIN JACK'S STRONGHOLD

Length: 2 miles round trip
Hiking time: 1.5 hours, day hike only
High point: 4,100 feet
Total elevation gain: 100 feet
Difficulty: moderate
Season: mid-April through mid-November
Water: none; bring your own
Map: USGS 7.5' Lava Beds National Monument
Permit: none required
Nearest campground: Indian Well Campground
Information: Lava Beds National Monument

This hike features highlights of both natural and human history. On the natural front, you'll observe interesting geological formations and gain expansive views of surrounding mountains. From the human history perspective, you'll learn about Captain Jack's Stronghold and why it was an important Modoc Indian War site.

Drive Lava Beds National Monument Road 13 miles northwest of

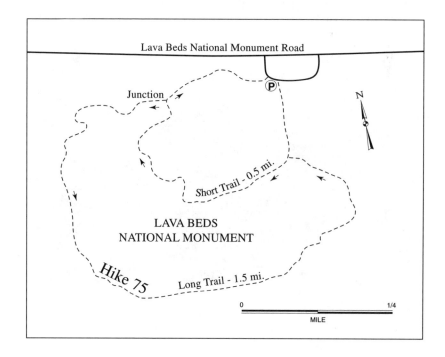

the visitor center (3.3 miles east of the Hill Road/Lava Beds National Monument Road junction) and park in the large lot on the south side of the road.

First, stop to read the sign that details the partial draining of Tule Lake to create farmland. Then, snag the brochure at the trailhead that gives detailed descriptions of the stronghold and the various events of military significance that took place here. (Look for the 21 numbered trailside posts.)

The path's paved portion soon ends, replaced by a lumpy rock tread that demands careful attention to foot placement. The typical plants of the region punctuate the half-mile-square lava field: sagebrush, rabbitbrush, antelopebrush, bitter cherry, mountain mahogany, western juniper, and a few specimens of fernbush.

Armed with the informative brochure, you're now ready to enter the stronghold itself. You'll pass sniper outposts, the main defense line, small caves used for shelter, and a medicine circle. Near post 10, you'll have excellent views. Look for Mount Shasta and Mount Dome to the west; Tule Lake and southern Oregon mountains to the north; the Warner Mountains to the east; and lava flows, numerous cinder cones, and the Medicine Lake volcano to the south.

Reach a trail fork at post 12. A right turn takes you back to the parking lot for a half-mile loop. Those wishing a more in-depth immersion in the stronghold should turn left for more views and visits to the last nine posts, which will entail a 2-mile hike.

Nearby: Lava Beds National Monument contains several other

Mountain mahogany is a large shrub or small tree that is a common resident of Lava Beds National Monument.

Modoc Indian War sites. Visit Hospital Rock (2 miles east on Lava Beds National Monument Road); Canby's Cross, where General Canby was assassinated by Modoc Indians during negotiations (2.7 miles west on Lava Beds National Monument Road); Gillem's Camp and Gillem Bluff (hike 74); and the Thomas-Wright Battlefield (hike 73).

Also be sure to visit Petroglyph Point. Indians carved over 5,000 symbols on the cliff and nearby rocks and caves. Some of the symbols could be as much as 4,500 years old. A brochure guides you on a short walk, giving you the opportunity to investigate the petroglyphs close-up. Bird-watchers will delight in observing the large community of cliff swallows and the numerous owls, falcons, and hawks that hunt here. To reach Petroglyph Point, drive east on Lava Beds National Monument Road 5.6 miles from Captain Jack's Stronghold (8.9 miles east of Hill Road), then go left and travel County Road 111 for 0.8 mile. Cross the railroad tracks, then follow signs and County Road 126 for the final 0.9 mile.

APPENDIX 1: INFORMATION

Almanor Ranger District
    Lassen National Forest
    P.O. Box 767
    Chester, CA 96020
    (916) 258-2141
Castle Crags State Park
    P.O. Box 80
    Castella, CA 96017
    (916) 235-2684
Eagle Lake Resource Area
    Bureau of Land Management
    2950 Riverside Drive
    Susanville, CA 96130
    (916) 257-0456
Hat Creek Ranger District
    Lassen National Forest
    P.O. Box 220
    Fall River Mills, CA 96028
    (916) 336-5521
Lassen Volcanic National Park
    P.O. Box 100
    Mineral, CA 96063-0100
    (916) 595-4444
Lava Beds National Monument
    P.O. Box 867
    Tulelake, CA 96134
    (916) 667-2282
McCloud Ranger District
    Shasta-Trinity National Forest
    P.O. Box 1620
    McCloud, CA 96057
    (916) 964-2184
McCloud River Preserve
    P.O. Box 409
    McCloud, CA 96057
Mount Shasta Ranger District
    Shasta-Trinity National Forest
    204 West Alma
    Mount Shasta, CA 96067
    (916) 926-4511
Recreation Department
    PG&E
    P.O. Box 277444
    Sacramento, CA 95826

APPENDIX 2: CAMPGROUNDS

Note that many campgrounds are closed from early autumn to mid-spring; call the information number for details if you hike outside the summer season. Also, you can camp in many parts of national forests and Bureau of Land Management lands as long as there are no signs forbidding it and you follow minimum impact guidelines. Obtain the road maps produced by these agencies, then head into the backwoods and find a nice, private spot near a dirt road.

AH-DI-NA CAMPGROUND
16 sites, fee, toilets, water. See directions for hike 56 (McCloud River Preserve) to reach the campground. For more information, call the McCloud Ranger District at (916) 964-2184.

AHJUMAWI LAVA SPRINGS STATE PARK
9 sites, fee (collected by roving attendant), toilets. Bring or purify your own water. See directions for hikes 46 through 48. For more information, call McArthur-Burney Falls Memorial State Park at (916) 335-2777.

BATTLE CREEK CAMPGROUND
50 sites, fee, toilets, water. Located 2 miles west of Mineral on Highway 36. For more information, call Almanor Ranger District at (916) 258-2141.

BIG PINE CAMPGROUND
19 sites, fee, toilets. Bring or purify your own water. Located on the east side of Highway 89, about 9 miles north of Lassen Park's north entrance and 4 miles south of the junction of Highways 89 and 44 East. For more information, call the Hat Creek Ranger District at (916) 336-5521.

BLACK ROCK CAMPGROUND
4 sites, fee, toilets. Bring your own water or purify Mill Creek water. Located at the hike 28 trailhead. For more information, call the Almanor Ranger District at (916) 258-2141.

BRIDGE CAMPGROUND
25 sites, fee, toilets, water. Located on the west side of Highway 89, about 17 miles south of Highway 299 and 4 miles north of the junction of Highways 89 and 44 East. For more information, call the Hat Creek Ranger District at (916) 336-5521.

BUTTE CREEK CAMPGROUND
14 sites, no fee, toilets. Bring your own water. Located just north of Butte Lake: Take Highway 44 east 11 miles from Highway 89, turn south at the road to Butte Lake, and drive 3 miles. For more information, call the Hat Creek Ranger District at (916) 336-5521.

CAVE CAMPGROUND

46 sites, fee, toilets, water. Located on the west side of Highway 89, just north of the junction of Highways 89 and 44 East and directly across from Subway Cave. For more information, call the Hat Creek Ranger District at (916) 336-5521.

CASSEL CAMPGROUND

27 sites, fee, toilets, water. Located just south of Baum Lake. See hike 40 for directions. For more information, write Recreation Department, PG&E, P.O. Box 277444, Sacramento, CA 95826.

CASTLE CRAGS STATE PARK

64 sites, fee, toilets, showers, water. Located on I-5's west side 48 miles north of Redding and 6 miles south of Dunsmuir (take the Castle Crags State Park exit). For more information, call the park at (916) 235-2684. Make reservations from May through September by calling 1-800-444-PARK.

CASTLE LAKE CAMPGROUND

6 sites, no fee, toilets, water. Located near Castle Lake; follow directions for hike 64. For more information, call the Mount Shasta Ranger District at (916) 926-4511.

FOWLERS CAMP CAMPGROUND

39 sites, fee, toilets, water. Take Highway 89 for 15 miles east of the junction of 89 and I-5 and 5 miles east of McCloud, turn south onto a dirt road signed for national forest river access and wildlife viewing. Follow signs for the final 0.7 mile. For more information, call the McCloud Ranger District at (916) 964-2184.

GUMBOOT CAMPGROUND

4 sites, no fee, toilets. Bring your own water. Follow directions given in hikes 65 and 66; the campground is 2.5 miles east of the trailhead. For more information, call the Mount Shasta Ranger District at (916) 926-4511.

GURNSEY CREEK

52 sites, fee, toilets, water. Located on Highway 36, about 3 miles north of the intersection of Highways 36 and 32. For more information, call the Almanor Ranger District at (916) 258-2141.

HAT CREEK CAMPGROUND

73 sites, fee, toilets, water. Located on the west side of Highway 89, about 12 miles north of Lassen Park's north entrance and 1.4 miles south of the junction of Highways 89 and 44 East. For more information, call the Hat Creek Ranger District at (916) 336-5521.

HOLE IN THE GROUND CAMPGROUND

13 sites, fee, toilets, water. Go 9 miles east of Mineral (or 9 miles northwest of the junction of Highways 32 and 36) on Highway 36 and

turn south on Highway 172. Go 3 miles to the town of Mill Creek, then turn left onto a dirt road that's 0.3 mile past Mill Creek Resort. Travel 2.8 miles to an intersection, then turn left for the campground located near the banks of Mill Creek. For more information, call the Almanor Ranger District at (916) 258-2141.

INDIAN WELL CAMPGROUND
40 sites, fee, toilets, water. Follow directions to the hike 69 trailhead. For more information, call Lava Beds National Monument at (916) 667-2282.

JUNIPER LAKE CAMPGROUND
18 sites, fee, toilets, water. See hike 17 for directions. For more information, call Lassen Volcanic National Park at (916) 595-4444.

MANZANITA LAKE CAMPGROUND
170 sites, fee, toilets, water. Located on Highway 89's west side, 33 miles north of the junctions of Highways 36 and 89 and 1 mile east of the junctions of Highways 44 and 89. For more information, call Lassen Volcanic National Park at (916) 595-4444.

MCARTHUR-BURNEY FALLS MEMORIAL STATE PARK
128 sites, fee, park entrance fee, toilets, showers, water. Located off Highway 89, about 6 miles north of the junction of Highways 89 and 299. For reservations (strongly recommended for period from Memorial Day through Labor Day), call 1-800-444-PARK. For more information, call McArthur-Burney Falls Memorial State Park at (916) 335-2777.

MCBRIDE SPRINGS CAMPGROUND
9 sites, fee, toilets, water. Located on Everitt Memorial Highway 5 miles from the town of Mount Shasta. Follow directions for hikes 49 through 52. For more information, call the Mount Shasta Ranger District at (916) 926-4511.

MERRILL CAMPGROUND
181 sites, fee, toilets, water. Located on the southern edge of Eagle Lake just off A-1, about 15 miles north of Highway 36. There are four other campgrounds nearby. For more information, call the Eagle Lake Ranger District at (916) 257-2151.

PANTHER MEADOWS CAMPGROUND
10 sites, no fee, toilets. Bring your own water. Located at the trailhead for hikes 49 through 51. For more information, call the Mount Shasta Ranger District at (916) 926-4511.

PIT RIVER CAMPGROUND
10 sites, no fee. Bring or purify your own water. Located near Pit 1 Powerhouse on the south side of Highway 299, about 3 miles west of Fall River Mills and 2 miles east of the Highway 299 bridge across Hat

Creek. For more information, call the Bureau of Land Management at (916) 233-4666.

SOUTHWEST CAMPGROUND

24 sites, fee, toilets, water. Located on Highway 89's east side, 6 miles north of the junctions of Highways 36 and 89, and 28 miles southeast of the junctions of Highways 44 and 89. For more information, call Lassen Volcanic National Park at (916) 595-4444.

SUMMIT CAMPGROUND

94 sites combined in the north and south sections, fee, toilets, water. Located on Highway 89's east side, 20.5 miles northeast of the junctions of Highways 36 and 89, and 13.5 miles southeast of the junctions of Highways 44 and 89. For more information, call Lassen Volcanic National Park at (916) 595-4444.

WARNER VALLEY CAMPGROUND

18 sites, fee, toilets, water. For directions, follow the route to the Boiling Springs Lake/Devil's Kitchen trailhead (hike 16). For more information, call Lassen Volcanic National Park at (916) 595-4444.

APPENDIX 3: WHAT TO TAKE

DAY-HIKE ESSENTIALS
  (from **Safety** section in the *Introduction*)
- adequate footwear
- compass
- day pack
- emergency signaling device
- fire starter (for wet wood)
- first-aid kit
- flashlight with extra bulb and batteries
- food
- knife (for kindling)
- maps
- matches
- pants
- poncho or space blanket
- sunglasses
- sunscreen
- sweatshirt
- toilet paper
- watchman's cap
- water
- water purifier
- wide-brimmed hat

OVERNIGHT EXCURSION ESSENTIALS
- items on day-hike essentials list
- air mattress or foam pad
- biodegradable soap
- dish scrubber
- extra underwear
- extra shirts
- extra socks
- extra pants
- 40-foot rope
- gloves
- hiking shorts
- lip protectant
- nylon or plastic ground sheet
- pot, cup, plate, bowl, spoon, fork
- pot holder
- rain gear
- sleeping bag
- small towel
- stove and fuel
- sturdy backpack
- sweater
- tent
- thermal underwear
- toothbrush
- warm jacket or parka
- watch
- waterproof pack covering

OPTIONAL ITEMS
- binoculars
- camera and film
- reading materials
- swimsuit

APPENDIX 4: FURTHER READING

Alt, David D., and Donald W. Hyndman. *Roadside Geology of Northern California*. Missoula: Mountain Press, 1975.

Bakker, Elna. *An Island Called California: An Ecological Introduction*. 2d ed. Berkeley: University of California Press, 1985.

Earthwalk Press. *Lassen Volcanic National Park: Hiking Map and Guide*. Eureka, Calif.: Earthwalk Press, 1987.

Kane, Phillip S. *Through Vulcan's Eye*. Lassen Volcanic National Park/ Loomis Museum Association: 1980.

Nelson, Raymond L. *Trees and Shrubs of Lassen Volcanic National Park*. Lassen Volcanic National Park/Loomis Museum Association: 1962.

Norris, Robert M., and Robert W. Webb. *Geology of California*. 2d ed. New York: Wiley and Sons, 1990.

San Diego Chapter of the Sierra Club. *Wilderness Basics: The Complete Handbook for Hikers and Backpackers*. 2d ed. Seattle: The Mountaineers, 1993.

Schaffer, Jeffrey P., et al. *The Pacific Crest Trail, Volume 1: California*, 5th ed. Berkeley: Wilderness Press, 1995.

Schulz, Paul E. *Road Guide to Lassen Volcanic National Park*. Lassen Volcanic National Park/Loomis Museum Association: 1990.

Schulz, Paul E. *Stories of Lassen's Place Names*. Lassen Volcanic National Park/Loomis Museum Association: 1949.

Selters, Andy, and Michael Zanger. *The Mt. Shasta Book*. Berkeley: Wilderness Press, 1989.

Showers, Mary Ann, and David W. Showers. *A Field Guide to the Flowers of Lassen Volcanic National Park*. Lassen Volcanic National Park/Loomis Museum Association: 1981.

Soares, John R. *Best Short Hikes in™ and Around the North Sacramento Valley*. Seattle: The Mountaineers, 1992.

Soares, John R, and Marc J. Soares. *100 Hikes in™ Northern California*. Seattle: The Mountaineers, 1994.

Stienstra, Tom. *California Camping*. San Francisco: Foghorn Press (updated yearly).

Stienstra, Tom. *California Fishing*. San Francisco: Foghorn Press (updated yearly).

Storer, Tracy I., and Robert L. Usinger. *Sierra Nevada Natural History*. Berkeley: University of California Press, 1963.

Whitney, Stephen. *A Sierra Club Naturalist's Guide*. San Francisco: Sierra Club Books, 1979.

Weir, Kim. *Northern California Handbook*, 2d ed. Chico, Calif.: Moon Publications, 1994.

Zanger, Michael. *Mt. Shasta: History, Legend & Lore*. Berkeley: Celestial Arts, 1992.

Note: Audubon Society Field Guides and the Peterson Field Guides provide a wealth of detail about plants, animals, and geology.

INDEX

ABOUT THE AUTHOR

John R. Soares is a writer and poet who lives in Chico, California. In addition to authoring numerous newspaper and magazine articles, he has written *Best Short Hikes In and Around the North Sacramento Valley* (The Mountaineers, 1992) and co-written *100 Hikes in™ Northern California* (The Mountaineers, 1994).

The author at the base of Castle Dome (Photo by Rick Ramos)

Other titles you may enjoy from The Mountaineers:

The *100 Hikes in*™ Series
Best-selling mountain hiking guides with fully detailed trail descriptions, directions, maps, and photos.
> *Northern California,* John R. Soares & Marc J. Soares
> *California's Central Sierra & Coast Range,* Vicky Spring
> *Arizona,* Scott S. Warren
> *Colorado,* Scott S. Warren
> *Oregon,* Rhonda & George Ostertag
> *Inland Northwest,* Rich Landers & Ida Rowe Dolphin
> *75 Hikes in New Mexico,* Craig Martin

The *Best Short Hikes in*™ Series
Popular hiking guides to spectacular surroundings for those with limited time and energy. Include distance, difficulty, directions, maps, and photos.
> *In and Around the North Sacramento Valley,* John R. Soares
> *California's Northern Sierra,* Karen & Terry Whitehill
> *California's Southern Sierra,* Karen & Terry Whitehill

California State Parks: A Complete Recreation Guide, Rhonda & George Ostertag
Part of best-selling *State Parks* Series. Profiles nearly 200 diverse recreation areas and the activities and amenities within them.

The High Sierra: Peaks, Passes, and Trails, R. J. Secor
Most complete guide available. Covers all known routes to approximately 570 peaks; details permit info, safety, and history.

THE MOUNTAINEERS, founded in 1906, is a nonprofit outdoor activity and conservation club, whose mission is "to explore, study, preserve, and enjoy the natural beauty of the outdoors. . . ." Based in Seattle, Washington, the club is now the third-largest such organization in the United States, with 15,000 members and four branches throughout Washington State.

The Mountaineers sponsors both classes and year-round outdoor activities in the Pacific Northwest, which include hiking, mountain climbing, ski-touring, snowshoeing, bicycling, camping, kayaking and canoeing, nature study, sailing, and adventure travel. The club's conservation division supports environmental causes through educational activities, sponsoring legislation, and presenting informational programs. All club activities are led by skilled, experienced volunteers, who are dedicated to promoting safe and responsible enjoyment and preservation of the outdoors.

If you would like to participate in these organized outdoor activities or the club's programs, consider a membership in The Mountaineers. For information and an application, write or call The Mountaineers, Club Headquarters, 300 Third Avenue West, Seattle, WA 98119; (206) 284-6310.

The Mountaineers Books, an active, nonprofit publishing program of the club, produces guidebooks, instructional texts, historical works, natural history guides, and works on environmental conservation. All books produced by The Mountaineers are aimed at fulfilling the club's mission.

Send or call for our catalog of more than 300 outdoor titles:

The Mountaineers Books
1001 SW Klickitat Way, Suite 201
Seattle, WA 98134
1-800-553-4453